Contents

The section 'Children working together' includes quick reference pages which describe some basic learning techniques. These are referred to in the rest of the text by an asterisk*.

Resources referred to in the text are either included in the resources lists at the end of the section; this is indicated thus †. Otherwise, they are referenced thus [1] in the annotated list on page112.

Summer 1990

Dear Anna,

Thanks for the letter and your enquiries about the Development Education Centre and the primary project. I'll try my best to answer.

The DEC is a small educational charity situated in Selly Oak Colleges. We have a particular interest in developing an international dimension in the curriculum. Most of our work is with teachers, right across the age range from nursery to F.E. Although we mainly work with Birmingham schools, we are developing strong partnerships with teachers in neighbouring authorities. Like many small organisations our funding comes from many different sources; part of the primary project has been funded by the City of Birmingham for a number of years now. The primary project began in 1983 as there was felt to be a real need for curriculum development in the primary sector.

One of the original aims of the project was to produce materials for theme work with a global dimension. I met with a group of enthusiastic teachers who beavered away for eighteen months - in their own time, discussing classroom practice, the role of attitudes, themes, whole school policies etc. We thrashed around lots of ideas which eventually formed the basis of the first edition of 'Theme work'. This was launched in February 1986 and subsequently a national conference was held for inservice providers.

Since then, I've spent quite a lot of time running further inservice courses, both school and centre based, on the ideas in 'Theme work' and the other two books in the series - 'Hidden messages?' and 'A sense of school'. One area in which teachers were interested was how to run inservice which involved all staff. Out of this, an idea gathered shape to produce a photopack of primary schools to discuss issues of the hidden curriculum. 'Behind the scenes' was duly published in 1988. We also revised another photopack 'Working now' which is designed for discussing gender roles at work.

More recently we have been looking at primary science and how we can develop a global dimension to that in the context of the national curriculum. A teachers group are writing up ideas in a publication for launch in early 1991. Another group have been looking at how to explore some of the key development issues in the world such as debt, trade, tourism etc. with upper juniors. They are using East Africa as a focus and visited Kenya and Tanzania for a month as part of an inservice course. A photopack arising from their work will also be available in early 1991.

We are continuing to do some work looking at development education in the early years. It's a vitally important area - but very difficult to fund at present.

Come and visit DEC sometime - we have a bookshop which stocks posters, handbooks, photopacks, childrens books etc. - in fact almost all the resources recommended in this book are in the shop and many more. It's worth a visit!

All the best,

Catherine

Theme Work

- a global perspective in the primary curriculum in the '90's

Cross curricular theme work offers tremendous potential for development education in the context of the national curriculum in the primary school. By organising themes imaginatively, we can create an environment in which children can begin to explore some of the issues surrounding them in the world today.

The original *Theme work* was published in 1986 as the result of some intensive work by a small group of primary teachers in Birmingham schools. The new, fully revised, edition has been written to take account of some of the changes and developments which have taken place in the interim period. A greater number of resources are available in the field of development education, multi-cultural/anti-racist education and in gender initiatives. The thinking in these and related fields has blossomed over recent years. New challenges are offered by the national curriculum and the Education Reform Act.

When teachers plan theme work together, there can be a dynamic creative sharing of ideas, resources and activities. The first part of this book suggests how the process of planning together might take place. We also discuss the process of learning and the value of group work. The section entitled 'Children working together' outlines some basic activities which can be applied in many different situations.

Four themes are used to illustrate how a global dimension might be developed with children. 'What is a country?' explores an understanding of place and the relationship between places. 'Roots and journeys' looks at how and why people travel and what they bring with them. 'Images' explores the role of perceptions in learning and suggests how children can begin to express and talk through their assumptions. 'Change' takes a concept focused approach in order to draw connections between how people's experiences change.

Many teachers who used the original *Theme work* extensively have contributed their expertise and experience in the development of this new book.

Catherine McFarlane.

Published and available from

Development Education Centre,
Selly Oak Colleges,
Bristol Road,
Birmingham B29 6LE

© **Development Education Centre [Birmingham] 1991**

ISBN 0 9506619 8 8

Development education - an insight from Kenya

As part of a study visit inservice course, set up by the Development Education Centre, a group of primary teachers from England visited Kenya and Tanzania for a month one summer. The purpose of the study visit was to meet with community groups, development workers, environmental organisations and others to experience a little of the life of people who live in two African countries. As a result of these experiences those teachers have put much thought into questions such as: What is development? How does development in the countries of the South relate to development education in British schools? What does development education look like in the primary school?

One of the most exciting things the group found about visiting community projects and particular women's projects was to see the similarity between the aims of development and development education in Britain. One Kenyan woman who works mainly with women's groups described how she was supporting Kenyan women in defining and meeting their own needs, as far as possible by relying on their own resources.

Because women in Kenya have traditionally had power in the area of family life, the project aims to encourage women to recognise and draw on this power. An *animator* is chosen from the community, who is given training in working with groups of people. The *animator* then returns to her community, brings the women together and spends time encouraging them, building their confidence and helping them to analyse their situation.

Together the women highlight what their needs are and decide how they might be able to meet them. There is often a temptation to initially look outside for help, but some needs can be met using the women's own resources and it is to these that the animator will guide the group first. Once they have defined their needs and acted on them, the group looks at what they have done and reflects on how it might be taken further.

This understanding of development relates closely to our understanding of development education; if development is about empowering people to make choices, to participate, to work together, then development education is about the processes which allow this to happen. Communities are not isolated, these issues facing a group of Kenyan village women may be similar to those facing groups of people in Manchester and Bangkok.

When people can see the similarities and links between their situations; when they know that the issues facing them are rooted in similar systems; when they are able to share some of their solutions and support each other, they begin to understand that development education is not only about participation and empowerment but it's about global literacy - understanding how communities, societies and the world operate.

As we describe in the next pages, development education in the primary school draws on these qualities of confidence and skill building, exploring and examining attitudes, participation, active and child centred learning, understanding the links between peoples, looking at issues and understanding different perspectives.

Dimensions of development education

'Development education, as it has developed in primary schools is fundamentally about a way of approaching things which will empower children to develop and express viewpoints and will heighten their awareness of the ways in which they are linked to other people, and our planet both locally and globally. Any content can be harnessed to this exploration, because it is the context in which this is set that is important and appropriate processes which will enable the development of skills and concepts.' [1]

Skill building

The kinds of issues which we are faced with are complex and continually changing. To help children to deal with them, we need to help them develop appropriate skills. These skills are an essential basis for collaborative and participatory work. We have found it valuable to concentrate on building up skills such as:

- *recognising our own attitudes and what influences them;*
- *building up empathy with people both in familiar and different situations;*
- *recognising that people hold different points of view;*
- *being confident in our own opinion and being able to argue ideas;*
- *being able to listen to other ideas;*
- *being critical of the information we are given.*

These skills cannot be taught in a didactic way; they have to be built up through practice, through talking, listening and debating in groups. In order to do this effectively, children will need to build up skills in group work itself. A discussion about these skills can be found on pages 32 and 33.

Examining attitudes

Most teachers are aware of the importance of attitudes in learning; as one teacher put it, 'it all boils down to attitudes, the child's attitudes and the teacher's'. Although attitudes can often simply be seen as a problem, their role in the learning process needs to be fully recognised.

This has been particularly clear when we teach about issues such as racism or why people are hungry. It is vital to recognise that children come with preconceived ideas which will affect how they understand new ideas. For instance, if a group of children receive negative racial stereotypes from their social environment, these are likely to affect how they learn about issues of immigration.

It is important to create a classroom environment which enables all children to recognise, express and explore their own attitudes and to understand attitudes of other people. In this kind of learning situation, we need to think about how to encourage children to challenge and affirm each other's attitudes. We also need to be clear about whether we are wanting the children to develop certain attitudes such as a sense of justice.

Exploring attitudes with any age group needs sensitive handling and small groups can often be beneficial. It has been shown that children are more likely to express attitudes when a teacher is not present and that quite early on they learn what is a 'right' or a 'wrong' attitude to express in school. [A fuller discussion of this can be found in *Children and Race, ten years on* [2]]. This then suggests that working in groups is the most appropriate way for children to express their attitudes and explore them. We also need to think about the influence of our own attitudes on how and what we teach.

Confidence building

An important part of the learning process is that of confidence building. To be able to work well together in a group, to be able to collaborate and share, children need to feel secure about themselves. Development education needs to encourage children's sense of identity and value.

Values and perspectives

People often view the world from very different starting points, for example, depending on where they have come from, their gender, their age, their ethnic or cultural background, their economic situation etc. People therefore make different judgements about what is going on in the world. These perspectives are not always obvious to others and can form the basis of a whole host of misconceptions. Children who learn about different perspectives on a given issue are more likely to appreciate that their way of viewing the world is only one amongst many.

Participation and responsiblity

It is important to have a supportive classroom environment which enables all children to participate and take responsibility for their learning. Pair or group work allows children to participate in learning. By giving them a specific task, they can become fully involved in the active learning process. Teachers who have enabled children to direct their learning have often seen in them a new found confidence and interest. The national curriculum affirms and supports specific skills which enhance children taking responsiblity for their learning, such as talk, listening, decision making etc.

Educational initiatives

Development education has much in common with anti sexist education, anti racist education, peace education, environmental education etc. Children need to become aware of the interdependence of the issues which they are raising. The context of current global developments makes these links all the more obvious and important to explore.

The global content

There is a place for recognising the children's own experiences but also for challenging them with new perspectives. Children tend to respond well to stimuli which reflect their own situations. This is especially true if their experience is not normally reflected in books, television etc. We need to ensure that we offer a child centred education, but not an education limited by the child's own experience, which might lead to unequal access to the curriculum.

It is also vital to bring in new experiences which will widen children's understanding of the world they live in. We all have links with other peoples and other parts of the world. You only have to look at the items in a shopping trolley to see the extent to which the world is interdependent. We should not only look at how the world is interdependent but also at the power relationships involved.

In order to be able to look at the concerns of people around the world, children need background information. Geographical and historical concepts and knowledge will be of particular value.

Issues

Controversy is part of life, outside and inside the classroom. Learning to respond thoughtfully to issues is an important part of growing up. These may be issues in the media, in the local community, or they might be the children's own issues and concerns. We would probably not want to rely on young children with limited experience for all topics, but they are likely to have genuine issues to define and discuss, e.g bullying in the playground. These can be powerful starting points for recognising that in any situation people have different points of view and different interests.

It is also important to introduce issues which will broaden the children's horizons and show the connections between their own issues and those of peoples in different parts of the world. Many of these issues can be developed in the national curriculum, in a cross curricular fashion, thus avoiding needless duplication.

it offers opportunities for addressing real issues

it builds on children's interests and concerns

it enables children to make links in their understanding of the world

children learning most effectively if it's for a real purpose - or solving real problems

its child centred but not child limited

it offers a real framework for children's learning

it breaks down artificial subject barriers - with a stress on links and connections

excellent for skills and concept development

it's a living, organic approach to learning

it reduces the stress of subject failure

it offers an antidote to "only for assessment" workplans

it avoids the duplication of skills learning

it's flexible and dynamic!

Why do theme work?

it's fun!

it encourages community links

all children have a chance to shine

it develops children's self esteem and confidence

children have more responsibility for the direction of their learning

education breaks out of the classroom

they can work at their own pace and learn from peers

it encourages equal access to the curriculum

parents become more confident about their involvement

group work changes roles

for girls, black, bilingual learners, those with special needs etc.

ownership leads to them naturally assessing and planning

it encourages a positive attitude to learning

An approach to the national curriculum

Cross curricular theme work can be a vehicle for innovative, child centred enquiry and debate, as well as a medium through which children can begin to understand the world around them. The national curriculum offers potential for these approaches.

In each of the national curriculum documents we find support for the organisation of contexts for children's learning across subject boundaries. Each supports an active approach, using talk and group work. Emphasis is laid on the importance of addressing controversial issues and ensuring that equal opportunities are central to the curriculum. The non statutory guidance suggests how this can be done in practice.

These statements from a range of DES and NCC documents support a cross curricular, development education approach to the national curriculum. The TGAT report [3] has pointed towards the importance of a cross curricular focus in any development of standard assessment tasks.

'Wherever possible, one or more [profile] components should have more general application across the curriculum; for these a single common specification should be adopted in each of the subjects concerned.'
Task group on assessment and testing:report [3] paragraph 35

'Courses should prepare students for teaching the full range of pupils and for the diversity of ability, behaviour, social background and ethnic and cultural origin that they are likely to encounter among pupils in ordinary schools....Students should learn to guard against preconceptions based on race, gender, religion or other attributes of pupils and understand the need to promote equal opportunities.'
Criteria for Assessment in Teacher Education [5] 6.3

'On completion of their course, students should be aware of the links and common ground between subjects and be able to incorporate in their teaching cross-curricular dimensions [e.g. equal opportunities, multicultural education and personal and social education], themes [e.g. environmental education, economic and industrial understanding, health education and the European Dimension in education] and skills [oracy, literacy and numeracy].'
Criteria for Assessment in Teacher Education [5] 6.2

'There will be a great deal of scope for teachers in schools to carry out curriculum development without cutting across the statutory requirements - indeed, the introduction of the National Curriculum seems likely to stimulate a lot of work at local level on aspects of the content of the curriculum and its organisation and to help focus this on the essentials of what teachers and pupils need... Making sure that such work by teachers can go on, and that good practice is picked up and spread, is essential to ensuring an up to date and valuable National Curriculum.'
From policy to practice [4] 5.4

'The foundation subjects are certainly *not* a complete curriculum; they are necessary but not sufficient to ensure a curriculum which meets the purposes and covers the elements identified by HMI and others. In particular, they will cover fully the acquisition of certain cross-curricular competencies: literacy, numeracy and information technology skills...The whole curriculum for all pupils will certainly need to include at appropriate [and in some cases all] stages:

*   careers education and guidance;
*   health education;
*   other aspects of personal and social education; and
*   coverage across the curriculum of gender and multicultural issues.'
From policy to practice [4] 3.8

'On completion of their course, students should be able to teach about controversial issues in a balanced way.'
Criteria for Assessment in Teacher Education [5] 6.4

'....it is never possible to divorce a community from its wider social context. To fully understand one's own community one must be aware of that wider context and of the complex inter-relationships that knot together humanity. An awareness of global concerns, those that affect all pupils as inhabitants of this earth, is thus implied automatically...We are just as determined as the noble Lords that these issues should be addressed and shall take steps to ensure that they are appropriately covered within the national curriculum. They will be dealt with in many subject areas.'
The Earl of Arran, Government spokesperson in the Lords on the Education Reform Bill [6].

Choosing a theme

Children learn skills, concepts and attitudes through imaginative combinations of themes offered in their primary education. There is scope for a creative approach in the context of the national curriculum.

In selecting a theme there are many things to think about. Your selection may be influenced by a spark that fires the class's imagination, your own interests or a set school curriculum plan. Whatever the reason for your choice, care needs to be taken to ensure every child's entitlement to a rich, broad, balanced and relevant curriculum. Positive provision needs to be made for girls, black learners, bilingual pupils and those with special educational needs.

1. Continuity and progression
The theme should provide a range of learning opportunities which build on the skills, attitudes or concepts which the children have already acquired and extend these.

2. A cross curricular approach
Children's learning crosses subject barriers and forms a cohesive whole. Since dividing the curriculum into subjects can inhibit the potential of children's learning, planning a theme should take account of a cross curricular approach.

3. Breadth and balance
Over each academic year children will need to experience a balanced curriculum; the choice of theme will therefore be influenced by what you have looked at earlier in the year and what you plan to do later. Some schools alternate a science focused theme with an historical, or geographical one. Other schools try to ensure that these dimensions are present in all themes.

4. Differentiation
Planning needs to ensure that the theme enables children to make appropriate progress at their own levels and to use the experience, skills and understanding they already have.

5. Relevance
If the theme is to be genuinely relevant to the children, it should offer opportunities to learn through direct experience, to draw upon and extend the children's knowledge and interests.

MMMM....
EDUCATIONALLY
EXCITING,
BUT WE ARE
RUNNING A
SCHOOL YOU
KNOW

Starting points
Although there are many possibilities for primary themes, some well worn favourites, such as *Autumn,* and *Ourselves* appear surprisingly often. The scope within such themes is vast, yet often a familiar format is adhered to. This common pool of experience can offer security - but it can also mean that little reference is made to the children's interests or needs. Choosing different titles for themes can help avoid this.

- How about using a question or a problem as a starting point, such as:
  What's the most efficient form of transport?
  Can we recycle it?
  What is happening to the rainforest?
  The children's own questions and concerns act as genuine starting points for theme work.

- Choose a title around a concept, such as *Interdependence* or *Conflict.* A list of concepts can be found on page 97.

- More unusual titles such as *Two square miles - the area around the school* or *Fire and light* or *Inside/outside* can offer new perspectives.

- Using a book as a starting point, offers endless possibilities as many children's books raise issues which can be explored in themes.

- Current issues in the news lend themselves to relevant and interesting themes. There is usually plenty of material available from items in the news which can also be used to build media skills.

- Issues which arise from everyday items can offer exciting starting points. The ideas on the opposite page suggest how to make an issue of an ordinary item such as box of matches, a chocolate creme egg or a deodorant spray.

- Juxtapose two theme titles, such as the environment and gender roles, or Roman Britain and human rights. This can often suggest new possibilties.

- Global connections can be drawn from any place or situation. If your annual class visit is to a castle, use this as your theme and draw out issues such as: Why did people have to defend themselves? What forms of protection did and do people use? Who were the invaders? Who is invading countries in the world today? What does it feel like to be under threat?

- Local community issues and concerns will motivate children's interests.

Issues and concepts

When themes are organised around content, children often forget the information they learn in a matter of weeks. The emphasis on content can be avoided by planning themes around concepts and issues.

Concepts are tools which children can use to organise their own understanding of the world. An open ended approach should be an integral part of concept based themes, as without this they can simply become another way of transmitting content. For instance, if the theme *Change* is taken as an example of a concept based theme and the teacher chooses to look at change in fashions, the end result may be a study of fashion. A further discussion about concepts can be found on pages 96 and 97.

1. Starting with content
Primary themes tend to be organised around areas of content e.g. *The Victorians* or *Electricity in the home.* This approach can be enhanced if the theme also concentrates on one or two concepts. For instance, the theme *The Victorians* might focus on cause and consequence as a key dimension.

2. Starting with concepts
Themes can also be organised around the idea of building up children's understanding of a concept. This probably means beginning with reflecting on the children's own experiences and then looking at wider experiences or situations. This approach is used throughout this book.

Making an issue of it
Try this activity, devised by Ange Grunsell and Theresa Stearn in your staff group to show that development issues fall within the framework of the national curriculum.

Divide into groups of three or four and give each group a piece of sugar paper, a felt pen and a different object such as a can of coca cola, a battery, a creme egg etc. Keep the price tags on. Each group should then write down every question they can think of to ask about the product; see the example below of the creme egg. Alternatively, brainstorm* all the issues the object raises for them. Ask groups to select three areas they have noted and then talk about how they would set about studying them in the classroom.

Organise the activities under curriculum subject headings e.g. science, maths, technology etc. and then refer to the national curriculum documents to see how their activities illustrate particular attainment targets and programmes of study. Talk through the outcomes of the activity, in order to show how whilst, for example, the science or history activities contribute to the understanding of the issue, they never provide the whole story, therefore a cross curricular approach is essential! You will also become aware of the duplication amongst some of the documents - and save yourself work!

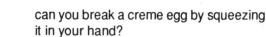

how many calories?

what is it made from?

where do the raw materials come from?

can you devise a fair test to see if the packaging is biodegradable?

do the growers get a fair price for their crops?

what other packaging could be used?

is cocoa and sugar grown by individual farmers or by large companies?

who invented creme eggs?

who manufactures it?

do the growers eat creme eggs?

can you find out about the company?

are they sold all the year round?
how are they advertised?

how long will a creme egg keep?

at what temperature does it melt?

how does the price of a creme egg compare with that of a real egg? which is more nutritious?

can you break a creme egg by squeezing it in your hand?

Planning

In planning themes, we need to be flexible enough to respond to children's interests but not be so loose as to be totally unstructured. Strategies for planning are suggested on the next few pages.

A commonly voiced fear about the national curriculum is that it will force a return to a subject centred approach. The evidence seems to be the opposite; teachers are so keen not to lose the good practice that they have built up in cross curricular work that there has been a focus of energy on looking at how this approach can be incorporated into the national curriculum initiatives. One of the welcome spin-offs of the national curriculum is that guidelines for thorough planning are being published by L.E.A.s and professional bodies.

The national curriculum - making it work for the primary school †

This excellent publication provides an overview of English, maths and science by showing how they are interrelated and offers a framework for whole curriculum planning. Practical grids for planning themes show how activities can be related to attainment targets and programmes of study. The grids ensure that knowledge does not become the overriding concern for teaching, so it becomes a vehicle for developing skills, attitudes and concepts. It shows how core subjects share common processes which relate to how children learn and to the way they work in the classroom. These processes include:

- Collaboration
- Exploring
- Investigating
- Making choices and deciding
- Organising
- Explaining
- Talking and communicating
- Sharing
- Observing
- Taking responsibility
- Asking and answering
- Recording
- Interpreting
- Predicting
- Recalling and reflecting

A checklist for planning

A number of considerations have to be borne in mind in planning themes. Opposite is a checklist of key questions which may help in your planning. To make it of greater personal value, add your own questions, reword those there and remove any which are not relevant. It is worth glancing at the checklist every so often when the theme is running to jog your own thinking.

Terms

Terms like theme work, environmental studies, topics and projects have been interchangeable. With the introduction of the national curriculum, we now have NCC cross curricular themes and NCC cross curricular dimensions, as well as subject areas. To avoid confusion in this book, we make the assumption that themes are broad based approaches to learning which draw on many if not all curriculum areas. We refer to those laid down by the National Curriculum Council as NCC cross curricular themes or NCC cross curricular dimensions.

NCC subjects
Core
English
Science
Mathematics

Foundation
History
Geography
Design and technology
Art
Music
Physical education

Religious Education

NCC cross curricular themes
Citizenship [individual, family, community, national, European and international including legal, and political dimensions]
Economic and industrial understanding
Health education
Environmental education
Careers education and guidance

NCC cross curricular dimensions
Multicultural education
Equal opportunities
Personal and social education
Special educational needs
Information technology

A checklist for planning

- Does the theme offer the children scope for:
  - considering issues
  - exploring values and attitudes
  - looking at perceptions and recognising points of view
  - looking at the experience of people outside their own cultures and society
  - making connections between themselves and the wider world
  - developing some key concepts
  - developing skills
  - challenging stereotypes
  - building empathy
  - effecting change
  - looking critically at sources of information
  - talking and listening
  - experiencing new ideas
  - building on personal experience
  - working collaboratively

- Are the children involved in the selection of the theme?

- Will they be involved in the planning and be responsible for the direction it takes?

- Does it take adequate account of the children's past learning experiences?

- How will you find out what the children know about the theme and what they bring to it?

- Does the theme draw appropriately on:
  - a range of curriculum areas
  - the NCC cross curriculum themes
  - the NCC cross curriculum dimensions

- How will the class record, present and evaluate what they learn?

- How will they be involved in evaluating their own work and the theme in general?

- Is the theme designed so all the children will have equal access to the curriculum?

- Is the theme broad and balanced?

- Will it encourage the bilingual children to use their home language/s ?

- Will the theme adopt a multisensory approach?

- Does it offer potential for developing real links with the local community?

- What opportunities for local visits and first hand experience does it provide?

- Does it offer a differentiated approach?

- Is it relevant and fun?

- What kind of creative timetabling is needed? Are there opportunities for collaborative teaching, cross phase links, cross year groups etc.?

A strategy for planning

Many schools already have their own ways of planning themes. The stimulus page opposite is designed to aid your planning and could be incorporated into your own particular process. It offers a process for making assumptions explicit and for checking that the work you have planned fulfills these. The steps on this page refer to the stages on the page opposite.

Step 1. Making assumptions explicit
Teachers have different ideas about what they are aiming to do by using themes in the primary classroom and often these assumptions remain implicit. When planning themes, it is important to make our assumptions explicit. The brainstorm* about the value of theme work on page 8 offers some of the assumptions underpining this publication. As a way of sharing assumptions, your staff group could do their own brainstorm*.

Step 2. Keep the children in mind!
Your own class will have specific interests, experiences, issues and needs which may contribute to the choice of the theme and the direction it takes. Are there ways the children can be genuinely involved in the planning? How will the theme build on what they have already done and how will extend their experience?

The 'What do you know? What do you want to know? activity'* on page 35 is a good starter.

Step 3. Decide on the theme
Some thoughts about selecting themes can be found on page 10. Be imaginative!

Step 4. Decide what specific things you want the children to gain from this theme
There are certain things we want children to gain from theme work in general, such as group work skills. However, from any particular theme there are likely to be specific things which we want children to concentrate on. These will include key concepts or skills and attitudes. Plan what you want the children to gain:

- in terms of attitudes and perceptions
- how to...........[skills]
- why?.............[concepts]
- what?.............[knowledge]
- others

By deciding what you want the children to gain, before looking at the attainment targets and programmes of study you will be designing a child centred, rather than a curriculum centred theme.

Step 5. Brainstorm* a web
Brainstorm a web of what the theme might cover, bearing in mind the children and what you want them to gain. This needs to be a selective brainstorm covering the areas which have most potential for work. How about making a web of questions to investigate, rather than content to cover?

Many brainstorms of topic webs become so extensive that they serve little purpose, other than to show the range of possibilities. When the web is focused, by taking into account the needs and interests of the children, the web becomes a more useful tool for planning.

Ask the children to brainstorm* what they would like to look at in the theme. Brainstorming questions to investigate rather than statements can encourage an enquiry based approach. Make your plans and the children's visible by putting them on the wall, this can help all to have a sense of theme.

Step 6. Check it out
At this stage, it is useful to review whether you are still on the track you started on. Look back at your assumptions in Step 1. Look at the checklist and review what you have done so far.

Step 7. In practice
This is a chance to look at methods and resources which you can use to develop the theme. This book focuses on four themes, but the methods and resources suggested can be used for many other themes. If the children are taking some responsibility for the planning, you will need to take this into account at this stage if not earlier. Sample the children's ideas after they have discussed and brainstormed and adjust your planning in view of this. Decide how the theme will flow, in particular how you are going to start it off.

Step 8. Evaluating and recording
You will need to ensure that what you have planned builds in opportunities for evaluation and recording, see pages 18 to 23.

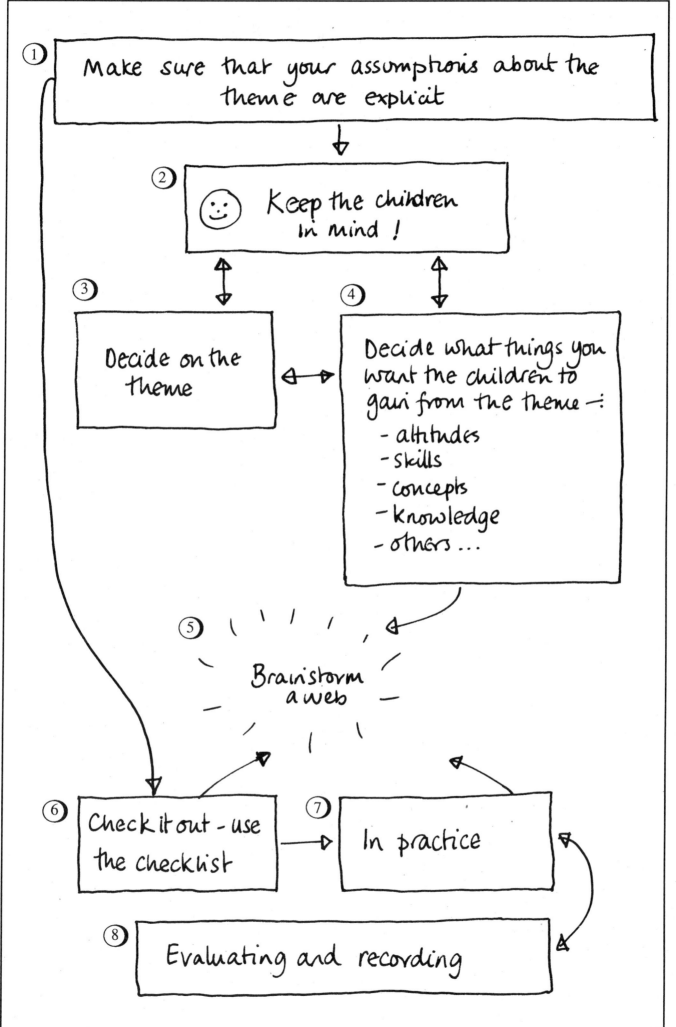

① Make sure that your assumptions about the theme are explicit

② Keep the children in mind !

③ Decide on the theme

④ Decide what things you want the children to gain from the theme —:
- attitudes
- skills
- concepts
- knowledge
- others ...

⑤ Brainstorm a web

⑥ Check it out - use the checklist

⑦ In practice

⑧ Evaluating and recording

15

A whole school approach

Working together as a whole school has all kinds of advantages. This is how one Birmingham school, developed a whole school approach.

The benefits of a whole school approach at Blakesley Hall results from an attempt to take control of our own future by developing an 'Integrated curriculum'. The national curriculum lies ahead with its heavy emphasis on subjects and stratification, the staff considered the need for a more manageable alternative which would support and develop all our children and teachers.

We believed the only way this could succeed was if there were a basic agreement in philosophy, a wide legitimation through ownership of the curriculum and thereafter an open sharing of expertise, planning, recording and development. Absolute meshing of views of course, was unlikely but it was heartening that we were able to establish an important philosophical platform.

The process begun in October 1987, is ongoing. Throughout this period when many schools suffered low morale concerning curriculum issues, the staff remained positive and created a framework which subsumed the national curriculum.

The integrated curriculum evolved through voluntary working parties co-ordinated by existing post holders. Interest was such that all staff devoted a great deal of time to many different groups and gained new insights to the whole curriculum across the primary phase. Having agreed on a basic child-centred direction, it was astonishing how well staff were able to break the infant-junior divide, acknowledge the continuum and maintain progression, balance and differentiation.

Frequent whole staff sessions sharing our work and alternating groups promoted good working relationships and team building. The curriculum related specifically to the needs of Blakesley children as well as local and national requirements because it grew out of the experiences of the staff. We now have nine skill areas, each divided into three levels covering the 4-11 age range; a bank of concepts and attitudes and a common format for forecasting and recording.

In integrating the curriculum, the massive overlap of skills in subject areas was apparent and in looking at the whole curriculum we were able to identify and synthesise these to avoid unnecessary repetition. Whether probationer or headteacher, we progressed together. Invaluable personal, professional and team development occurred.

Collaboration continues as national curriculum documentation is tagged into the integrated curriculum and in our termly planning and recording. The latter is achieved in self-supportive year group teams where the whole exercise is much more interesting, stimulating and worthwhile.

Year groups meet frequently, formally and informally to review progress and share resources. Collaborative teaching occurs across classes, years and phases. Experienced and inexperienced teachers learn together and are able to reflect meaningfully on the progress of the children and evaluate the developing curriculum. This is far more enlightening than the days of the isolated teacher in the 'closed' classroom.

All termly planning is open to examination on the staffroom noticeboards enabling further cross fertilisation of ideas between year groups and this documentation together with records is passed on to subsequent class teachers.

Our emphasis on the skills, concepts and attitudes is guiding the school towards a much more 'active', 'doing' practice and the collaborative process is enabling us to re-examine how we resource the curriculum. We are now in a position to sit down as a whole staff to prioritise our curriculum needs and to consider what every classroom or year group needs. This leads to a more democratic and effective sharing of resources.

Once we had started along this road, a dynamic was created now largely self-perpetuating and created a climate of reflection and learning. In examining the whole curriculum, agreeing a basic philosophy and creating a new framework subsequent developments are given a real place. Our current work concerns the creation of conceptually based themes with which to deliver the curriculum. We continue to acknowledge and value the expertise of the whole staff promoting a more legitimate way forward.

Peter Humphreys
Blakesley Hall Primary School

16

A whole school theme

A whole school approach can take many different forms. Blakesley Hall went in for all round change, but there are many other possibilities. One of these is to work on a whole school theme for a term or half term, in which all the classes work on the same theme. This page describes some of the possibilities and limitations.

Limitations

* A theme can become an artificial vehicle for learning if it is too contrived and does not respond to the needs of the class. Don't try and squeeze everything into your theme!

* Spontaneity is a key element of primary learning and theme work should not be too rigid.

* A theme can be imposed by one or two teachers and not have arisen out of a consensus.

* Schools need the flexibility to follow whole school themes when they want to and for classes to follow their own choices at other times.

* There can be a demand on the same resources.

Possibilities

* A common theme encourages a staff team to plan together. It also may open the door for collaborative teaching opportunities. Teachers feel more competent to do this if they have shared in the planning of a common theme.

* At a time when teachers are feeling insecure, for instance around the introduction of a new curriculum, shared planning can help create a supportive atmosphere.

* It helps the children to feel part of a whole school. Five year olds can feel very distant from eleven year olds; looking at the same theme could encourage more communication and liaison between different age groups. Assemblies can form a focal point for this.

* It helps develop a coherence of curriculum planning so that the same themes are not covered year in, year out, so that skills and concepts are developed progressively throughout the years in a planned way.

* A common theme is a great opportunity for organising a central collection of resources. This might encourage teachers to experiment with new stimuli e.g. cartoons, artefacts, photographs.

Evaluating and recording

The next four pages reflect on evaluation and recording classroom work. The lesson evaluation on page 21 has been developed in Manchester schools in evaluating 'World studies'[7].

The nature of theme work can make it difficult to record and evaluate in a common, structured way. Personal impressions of what has taken place are important sources but also need to be supported by more concrete evidence. An excellent resource which explores the practicalities of assessment in an accessible form is *Teacher assessment*†. A group of teachers discussing these issues came up with the following reasons for evaluating and recording:

- It is important to stand back and review what has been going on in a more detached way.

- Records of children's work are needed to assess progress. They serve as important sources for children and parents to see how they are getting on.

- They can help clarify what has been happening, what has been learnt and reactions to that.

- Evaluation enhances children's opportunities to take greater responsibilty for their own learning.

- Evaluation can show up strengths and weaknesses and highlight where support is needed for individual needs.

- Evaluation by teachers and children together can enhance relationships and learning potential.

Recording

The emphasis on active learning methods, talk and shared writing has implications for how children can most effectively record what they have experienced and done. The role of talk is increasingly recognised as having an important part to play in learning. The National Oracy Project has contributed to developing thinking and practice in the place of talk. Talk plays a prominent part across the national curriculum.

In designing appropriate strategies for evaluating and recording talk, we need to be clear that talk in itself is a valuable learning medium whether or not any record is kept. We also need to be aware that recording can itself influence the quality of the talk. Tape recording groups talking can give a useful insight into how children interact, as long as children are at ease with the machine. Tape recorders can have an advantage over the teacher whose presence might influence the talk to a greater extent!

Taking photographs of children working can also be a useful way of recording what has been taking place, especially if you can use them with the children to discuss how it went. Children can discuss some of the questions around the photograph here.

It is important that the non recorded aspects of learning are valued by parents, children and teachers as much as the recorded ones. This is particularly true in a climate in which some pieces of work will be assessed and others will not.

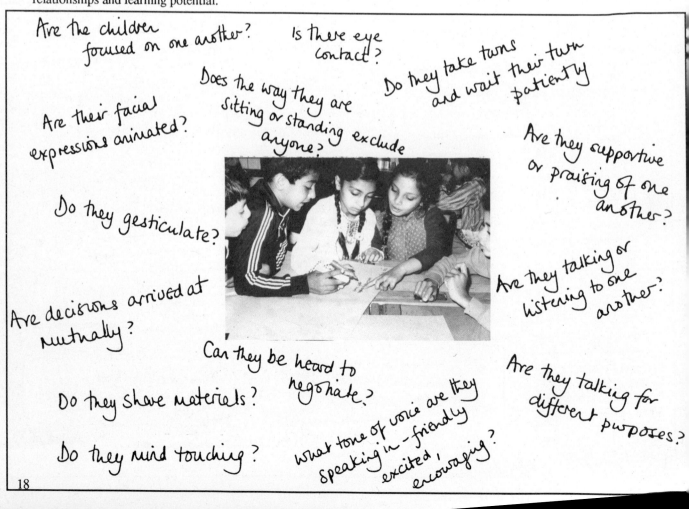

Are the children focused on one another?

Is there eye contact?

Does the way they are sitting or standing exclude anyone?

Do they take turns and wait their turn patiently

Are their facial expressions animated?

Are they supportive or praising of one another?

Do they gesticulate?

Are decisions arrived at mutually?

Are they talking or listening to one another?

Can they be heard to negotiate?

Do they share materials?

Are they talking for different purposes?

What tone of voice are they speaking in — friendly, excited, encouraging?

Do they mind touching?

What have I done?

It is not always possible or desirable for children to record the details of what they have done in groups. The strategies outlined here place emphasis on recording what the children have been exposed to, rather than the outcomes.

- Give each child a file in which to record each activity they do. This may amount to a couple of sentences describing it or a brief reflection on how it went or what they learnt.

- Give each child a sheet of different skills and ask them to put a tick by each skill when they have used it. Alternatively, they could colour a square next to the skill. These could include listening, discussing, recording, asking questions, finding information etc.

- Children could keep a daily diary of what they have done, in brief note form and discuss this once a fortnight with the teacher.

- Some classes are experimenting with learning logs which are daily or weekly diaries, everyone fills them in at a given time including the teacher. This could be at a random time in each week. They can be the private possession of the child or they can be books which are shown to teachers and parents for them to add their own comments.

Records for a purpose
Children may want to share what they have done with a wider audience, for example, their friends, other members of the school etc. These may take the form of class presentations in assemblies, whole class books, photographs, displays and exhibitions.

Profiles
Profiles can be an valuable way of evaluating and recording children's work. They can take many forms but all concentrate on the progress and experiences of the whole child, not just their academic success. Children become partners in monitoring their own progress. Reports might be written by the teacher and child together, or by the teacher in negotiation with the child. *The primary language record* † and *Patterns of learning*† offer very useful suggestions for profiling in the English curriculum.

Children can build up their own profile folder of a selection of their work. Clipped to each piece could be a brief comment by the child about:

- *how the work was produced [was it an individual or group piece; was it a draft or final piece etc.];*
- *why they chose it;*
- *what they thought of it;*
- *their reflections on the process of work.*

Teachers and parents can also add their comments. Instead of the traditional 'parent's evening'; invite both children and parents to discuss the children's profiles together.

Children will often need to learn skills in how to evaluate what they have done. It may be easy to rely on superficial judgements such as how neat it looks, which are standards and crtieria by which teachers have assessed in the past.

Communicating with parents
Parents are not always well informed about what their child is learning and this can lead to uncertainty, insecurity and poor relationships between home and school. Involving parents as partners in their children's education has to begin at the minimum with communication about what is going on in the school. This can be a starting point for building more fruitful relationships between parents and school. These are a few initiatives which schools have taken:

- Invite parents into school at the beginning of term to explain what is going to happen in the curriculum.

- Invite parents to a briefing about the national curriculum.

- Send home plans of what the children are going to do that term with space for parents to comment and add their ideas.

- Put the web of ideas about the theme on the classroom door or at the places where parents wait to pick up their children to inform them what is going on. One school which did this found that there were all kinds of offers from parents which would enhance the theme.

These kinds of initiatives have a number of spin-offs. It is likely that parents' interest, understanding and contribution to the curriculum will grow and their confidence in the school will increase.

Communicating with colleagues
When children go into a new class, some records of what the class have done usually travel with them. One staff team began experimenting with sending topic webs and plans of work. They marked with a fluorescent pen the work which they had covered and with another colour work they had hoped to cover but didn't.

PATTERNS OF LEARNING
The Primary Language Record and
The National Curriculum

How did it go?

These activities can be used to support children in evaluating their response to an activity.

Thumbs up

Conclude a lesson with a quick informal evaluation such as this one. Children who liked the activity put their thumbs up, those who disliked it put their thumbs down and those who were unsure put their hands flat.

Quick lesson evaluation

After an activity the class could sit in a circle and give a response to an open ended sentence such as:

What I liked about this afternoon's work was......
What I did not like about this afternoon's work was......
One thing I learnt this afternoon was......

This helps the children to clarify for themselves what they have learnt, so it is also confidence boosting. Alternatively, if it is threatening to go round a circle, you could try the same thing in groups or pairs, or as a class brainstorm.

Brainstorming

Before a project begins ask groups to brainstorm quickly as many words as they can about the new theme. The contributions can be collated from different groups to see what the overall knowledge and assumptions are of the class. Again, this could be referred to at the end of the project.

Smiley faces

A simple activity is to ask the children to draw a smiley face on their work if they enjoyed doing it or a grumpy face if they didn't.

Before and after questionnaire

Children could be given a questionnaire at the beginning of a project asking what they think or know about that particular theme. At the end of the theme they could fill in another copy of the questionnaire, compare it with their first one and discuss their findings in groups. Fill it in six months later to see what the sustained learning has been.

Stars

Ask the children to list the activities they have done at the end of the day or at the end of the week. Ask them on their own to give between one and four stars to each activity; one star means not very enjoyable, four stars means very enjoyable. Then share their starrings with a friend who has done similar activities and discuss their findings.

Group work

It is valuable for children to talk about the process of their group interactions. Suggestions for children evaluating their own group work can be found on page 30.

Debate

A debate at the end of some work could help clarify the children's understanding. It might also help the teacher to think about group work skills or discussion skills.

Key questions for evaluating your teaching

Before the lesson:

Record your objectives for the lesson.

Afterwards, ask these questions:

1. What did the children actually do ?

2. What were they learning i.e. knowledge, skills, attitudes?

3. How was it worthwhile ? [i.e. long term, short term goals and in terms of development and satisfaction]

4. What did I/we do ?

5. What did I/we learn ?

6. What did I/we intend to do ?

What does your classroom look like?

- Does the layout of the classroom encourage children to work together?

- Does it allow children to resource themselves - do they know where things are kept? Can they get easy access to glue, scissors, pens etc?

- Is the teacher's desk the focal point of the room?

- Are there areas where children can go and get on with something they are interested in?

- If there are classroom rules, who has made them and how far have they been negotiated?

- Who decides on what is displayed? Who does the displaying? How often is it changed?

- Does the layout of the room ever change? If so when, how often, by whose choice?

- Is there scope for children to follow their own avenues of interest?

- Is the school day organised to give all children maximum scope for developing at their own pace?

- Who decides what is learnt or taught?

- Are children involved in planning, recording and assessing their own work?

- Is there time for the teacher to stand back and watch what is going on?

- Are parents and other visitors welcomed?

The hidden curriculum

School ethos is as important as the philosophy and practice of the formal curriculum. The messages and values of the school and classroom have an impact on what children actually learn there. We need to recognise that the hidden curriculum is a powerful force in our children's education.

Children from an early age are not slow to pick up any mismatch of messages between what is said and what is done; the lessons of the classroom and the values of the school. Many will be aware, from a very early age of the school rules, the status of ancillary staff, the way parents are viewed, the assumptions made in the dining hall, the playground, the corridors etc. They will be aware of power relationships between children and adults and amongst adults who work in schools.

These values are often viewed as the norm, the ways schools as institutions operate. The damaging effects that various features of school life can have on particular groups of children for example, black children, girls, travellers etc. have now been extensively documented. There is overwhelming evidence that the real values of a school, expressed in its overall practice do influence children's learning and achievement. Equally, there is growing evidence that children's learning is enhanced in schools which are seeking to engender a co-operative ethos, where all children are given access to the curriculum, and for example where parents are viewed as partners in children's education.

The hidden curriculum is therefore a very powerful force in our children's education. If we are to take development education seriously in the primary school, we need not only address issues of power, justice, interdependence, bias etc. in the classroom but also look at how these are reflected in the context of the school.

The photopack, *Behind the scenes* [8] has been designed for use with staff groups to stimulate discussion about the context of the school. Examples of the photographs are shown here. The photographs show a range of school situations including classrooms, the playground, celebrating festivals, wall displays, staff meetings etc. The accompanying booklet contains ideas for exploring the hidden curriculum with your own colleagues. Using photographs of situations which are unknown yet familiar can help avoid the discussion becoming too personal.

There are clearly many areas which you could look at as part of this process of examining the hidden curriculum. A fruitful starting point can be to look at your own classroom.

What does your classroom look like?
It is a pattern that classrooms in which children take some control over their own learning, tend to be organised in such a way as to encourage the practice which they are seeking to promote. It is often possible to tell from the layout of the classroom whether children really have a say. The checklist opposite is one you could use as a starting point for thinking about classroom organisation. You might like to add your own questions to the end of it.

A chapter entitled 'A whole school approach; world studies and equal opportunities' in *Making global connections*[9] addresses how staff groups can begin to look at the ethos of their school. Practical strategies and comments from staff groups involved in this work make it readable and relevant. *"Where it really matters..."*† looks at issues of racism in primary schools and contains useful materials for staff groups. *"Can I stay in today, Miss?"*† offers strategies for significantly changing behaviour in the playground and suggestions for redesigning to make a child-friendly layout.

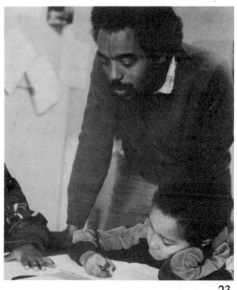

23

Resources: General reading

Art against apartheid, art and cross curricular activities for upper primary and middle schools, Janie Butler, Art and Development Education 5-16 project, 1990.
A practical and thought provoking handbook for raising issues about South Africa with children through art. The strategies can also be applied to other issues and themes.

"Can I stay in today, Miss?" improving the school playground, C. Ross and A. Ryan, Trentham books, 1990.
Bullying in the playground causes distress to many children and may damage their education and future opportunities. This practical handbook offers strategies for changing behaviour in the playground, reducing aggression and abuse. The strategies range from classroom activities to redesigning the entire playground.

Developing topic work in the primary school, Sarah Tann, The Falmer Press, 1988.
This book examines the role of topic work in the primary school by presenting case studies in which children, parents and teachers are partners in choosing, developing and monitoring theme work.

Earthrights, education as if the planet really mattered, Greig, Pike and Selby, WWF/Kogan Paul, 1987.
This publication explores the challenge of the global perspective to environmental education. It contains both theory and practical ideas.

Equal opportunities in schools: new dimensions to topic work, George Antonouris and Jack Wilson, Cassell, 1989.
A useful guide to the theory and practice of an equal opportunities approach to topic work. Examples of activities teachers have used are set out, with clear reference to resources and addresses.

Making global connections, a world studies workbook. ed. David Hicks and Miriam Steiner, Oliver and Boyd, 1989.
Chapters contain issue based material and classroom activities. They focus on Forest Environments, Aboriginal perspectives, Gender issues, Recycling and Food. The final section looks at a whole school approach and issues of evaluation.

Mathematics for all, ESG Project Salisbury, 1988.
Maths is a universal subject, yet it is by no means standard or uniform. This practical handbook opens our eyes to the variety of approaches and assumptions which underpin mathematics in other cultures.

The national curriculum - making it work for the primary school, Association for Science Education, 1989.
Produced by four subject associations, this book promotes ideas for planning cross curricular work in the context of the national curriculum. The processes set out will give confidence to teachers about integrating the main skills in the core subject areas.

Patterns of learning, the primary language record and the national curriculum, ILEA - CPLE, 1988.
A new and exciting document which looks at a process of recording language development in the context of the national curriculum for English. It presents a genuine, well thought out attempt to take account of bilingual developments. Very practical with a clear rationale.

Pedagogy of the oppressed, Paulo Freire, Penguin, 1972.
In his model for education, Freire advocates students and teachers learning together. He challenges the 'banking' approach to education whereby the students become receptacles for knowledge transmitted by teachers.

Teacher assessment, making it work in the primary school, Association of Science Education, 1990
A practical look at the process of developing effective assessment in the context of the national curriculum. This booklet offers a variety of views and approaches as the writers put themselves in the position of a school staff trying to decide on an assessment policy.

Topic work 3-13, National Primary Centre, 1990.
A folder of loose leaf sheets looking at issues for planning, managing, assessng, evaluating topic work in the primary school. Very accessible and down to earth.

A sense of school - an active learning approach to inservice, DEC, 1986.
Long term change will only happen if the whole school works through its policies together. This handbook, for those planning and facilitating inservice, encourages people to share ideas and work collaboratively.

Science with a global dimension, DEC, 1991.
This forthcoming publication is written by a group of primary teachers. The book takes four themes: wind, soil, shelter and food and through each addresses how children can begin to understand these issues in a global context. Sections on basic science approaches and inset are also included.

"Where it really matters.." - developing anti-racist education in predominantly white primary schools, DEC, 1990.
An innovative teachers' handbook outlining the rationale behind an anti-racist approach to primary education. Practical ideas for staff groups and classroom practice.

World studies 8-13, a teacher's handbook, Simon Fisher and David Hicks, Oliver and Boyd, 1985.
A handbook designed to help teachers plan themes with a global dimension. It contains some interesting classroom activities and can be used as suggested or as a stimulus for developing your own ideas. Updated in 1989.

Children working together

This section is concerned with the process of learning. Suggestions for organising group work are offered alongside some basic active learning approaches which can be developed in a variety of ways and applied to different situations.

To save repetition, we have included these approaches here in a simple form for quick reference. An asterisk* is used in the themes sections to refer to activities outlined in this one.

What do we mean by group work?

Development education is concerned with raising awareness and enabling children to build up skills to explore some of the complexities of a given situation. Group work gives scope for building the necessary skills, exploring attitudes and investigating issues. It is a dynamic and interactive process as summed up in Jane Sprackling's definition [1]:

'Co-operative group work is children working experientially in pairs or larger groups. The task that they are working on could have a structured goal, or could be open ended, but it must involve the skills of communication, and the children working as a team. There may, or may not be an 'end product'. Co-operative group work must be flexible in that it can be entirely cross-curricular.'

In the national curriculum

Collaborative group work processes can be applied to each curriculum area. They are most explicitly addressed in the national curriculum in the English document, although this clearly states that all activities should:

'draw on examples from across the curriculum, and in particular those existing requirements for mathematics and science which refer to use of spoken language and vocabulary, asking questions, working in groups, explaining and presenting ideas, giving and understanding instructions.'
English in the National Curriculum, Programme of Study 4, Key stage 1.

Other national curriculum documents also promote active learning styles. The science non statutory guidance, for example, states that questioning is an important skill.

Questioning may:

*   lead children to review ideas;
*   promote investigations;
*   demand detailed observation;
*   ask children to stop and rethink;
*   ask children to justify action or ideas;
*   encourage self criticism;
*   provide information on the child's understanding.
Non statutory guidance for science, 8.2

Children should also be able to:

*   divide into groups [where group work is appropriate];
*   agree upon individual responsibilities;
*   decide upon objectives [what to do and how to do it];
*   carry out tasks;
*   collect data;
*   analyse and interpret;
*   evaluate and draw conclusions;
*   communicate to others.
Non statutory guidance for science, 7.11

In mathematics, similar ideas underpin the non statutory guidance; it suggests that:

Children should develop skills in:

*   selecting materials and mathematics appropriate for a particular task;
*   planning and working methodically;
*   checking for sufficient information;
*   reviewing progress at appropriate stages;
*   checking that results are sensible;
*   using trial and improvement methods;
*   trying alternative strategies;
*   completing a task;
*   presenting alternative solutions.
Non statutory guidance, Using and applying mathematics 1.4

They should also develop ideas of argument and proof:

*   asking the question 'what if.....';
*   making and testing predictions;
*   making and testing statements;
*   generalising, making and testing hypotheses;
*   following arguments and reasoning and checking for validity;
*   conjecturing, defining, proving and disproving.
Non statutory guidance, Using and applying mathematics 1.4

Group work

Talk is a natural part of everyday life; it is an important vehicle for communication. It is through talking and listening that we can begin to explore unfamiliar ideas and can begin to clarify what we think.

Talk can open our minds so we think for ourselves. It allows us to draw on our own experience and ideas and hear of new experiences and perceptions. It is not surprising, therefore, that many of the literacy campaigns set up in the countries of the South are associated not only with reading and writing, but also with opening up people's minds.

It is encouraging to see the emphasis laid on talk in the national curriculum, in the English document and across the curriculum. These two quotations from the non statutory guidance for English give a flavour of this:

'In the early stages of particular projects, it will be important to give children the opportunity to explore for themselves unfamiliar ideas and to make their own connections. In talking with children, the teacher will need to ensure that questions are genuinely open-ended, children have problems to solve without a subtly indicated, expected answer and that they are encouraged to speculate, hypothesise, predict and test out ideas with each other and with the teacher. The emphasis needs to be on language being used, not to communicate what is known, but as an instrument of learning. It is time for children to think aloud, to grapple with ideas and to clarify thoughts.' [POS 2, 3 and 4]
Non statutory guidance for English, Key stage 1 - 4.2

'Once children develop their understanding of new ideas, they will need to reflect and exchange ideas and views with each other and with the teacher in order to consolidate learning. In addition, talk of this kind will provide the teacher with a check on the quality of understanding.'
Non statutory guidance for English, Key stage 1 - 4.4

Group work is an excellent vehicle for encouraging effective talk in the classroom. If structured well, it can offer a task some boundaries but also space in which children can talk through ideas and begin to take responsibilities for the direction of their own learning.

Angela Martin

The programmes of study for key stages 2 to 4, which support attainment target 1 illustrate the importance of talk:

Pupils should be given the opportunity to learn how to:
- express and justify feelings, opinions and viewpoints with increasing sophistication;
- discuss increasingly complex issues;
- assess and interpret arguments and opinions with increasing precision and discrimination;
- present their ideas, experiences and understanding in a widening range of contexts across the curriculum and with an increasing awareness of audience and purpose;
- ask increasingly precise or detailed questions;
- present factual information in a clear and logically structured manner in a widening range of situations - discriminate between fact and opinion and between relevance and irrelevance, and recognise bias;
- use, and understand the use of, role-play in teaching and learning, e.g. *to explore an aspect of history, a scientific concept or a piece of literature;*
- communicate with other group members in a wide range of situations, e.g. *an assignment in mathematics where a specific outcome is required;*
- discuss issues in small and large groups, taking account of the views of others, and negotiating a consensus;
- report and summarise in a range of contexts;
- reflect on their own effectiveness in the use of the spoken word;
- engage in prediction, speculation and hypothesis in the course of group activity.

The range of opportunities provided should:
- not be restricted to English lessons but be available across the curriculum;
- allow pupils to work in groups of various size, both single sex and mixed where possible, with and without direct teacher supervision;

Why is group work important for children?

For effective learning
Group work promotes more efficient learning than competition or individuation. It encourages the creative sharing and generating of ideas.

For working together
Learning can be too individualised, so it is important to develop opportunities for working together. Through group work children can develop skills of self confidence, communication and co-operation. Small groups maximise opportunities for building skills.

For open ended learning
Although a task or stimulus may be the focus of group work these methods offer opportunities for children to explore areas they are interested in at their own levels. They allow children to take more responsiblity for and control over their own learning.

For confidence building
It takes confidence to share opinions or ideas in a class discussion - group work can help children to test out their thoughts on others and clarify their ideas. Talk is a very valuable medium for sorting out your own ideas.

For building on enthusiasm
Children enjoy participating.....in assemblies hands shoot up when volunteers are needed. Group work, which involves being active for a large proportion of the time, is an opportunity to respond to their enthusiasm and motivation.

For learning to value their own experiences
All children come to school with a wealth of experience. They need to learn that they have important things to say and share with others.

For promoting equal opportunities
Children with special needs may be catered for by creating different sorts of groups and partnerships. A bilingual child may have more opportunity to contribute in a mother tongue group when operating in a language which gives greater meaning. Girls may benefit from sometimes working in single sex groups.

The teacher's role

Group work encourages children to interact with and learn from each other. Learning situations which are child centred and directed have implications for the the role of the teacher.

It is inevitable that group work will change the role of the teacher. The emphasis will be on setting up learning situations and drawing out ideas from the children. The teacher will have a little more interaction time with individuals; the children will learn from each other.

In covering the programme of study for Speaking and Listening in the national curriculum, it is stated that the teacher should be:

- helping to sustain what children are trying to say by showing interest;
- an exploratory user of language;
- supportive and encouraging to the children in their use of language;
- able to create an atmosphere of challenge and involvement;
- prepared to intervene only when it is appropriate;
- aware of the special needs of speaking impaired and/or hearing impaired children;
- sensitive to individual needs, especially when the child is shy or lacking confidence;
- aware of the need to make the verbally aggressive or dominating child sensitive to others;
- aware of the need for bilingual children to work with others in their home language and in English, to strengthen their capacity to use English for a range of purposes;
- prepared to monitor and evaluate the collaborative use of spoken language.

Non statutory guidance for English, Key stage 1 5.1

Recent research by teachers involved in the National Oracy Project [2] has shown that children need space to interact and do things together without the presence of a teacher. This in itself can sometimes limit the quality of their learning. In inservice courses about group work, teachers regularly assume that group work involves one adult working with each group of children. This leads to the misconception that group work can only take place if most of the class are occupied so that the teacher is left to work with a group.

If everything is working well in the classroom with the minimum of teacher intervention, it may be possible to stand back and watch and listen to the children. Often there seems to be little time for what might seem like the luxury of observation and reflection, but even short bursts will be of great value in understanding what is happening and ascertaining the next stage of development.

When opportunities arise for collaborative teaching, teachers can act as strong role models for the class. Further discussion of this can be found in *Shared learning†*. Using group work can also challenge our expectations of children. In workshops where teachers discussed how children respond to an activity, many have been surprised by the sophistication with which their children have approached ideas.

An enquiry based teacher
In *World Studies 8-13* [3] Fisher and Hicks outline some characteristics for teachers who are interested in setting up 'enquiry-based' learning situations. The teacher:

- *rarely tells pupils what they 'ought' to know;*
- *is mainly interested in helping pupils learn to learn;*
- *stresses, by example, that education is a process of finding answers;*
- *uses questioning as a basic strategy with pupils;*
- *encourages openness to alternative perspectives, explanations and ideologies and rarely accepts one viewpoint as the single answer;*
- *encourages pupil-pupil interaction as opposed to solely pupil-teacher interaction;*
- *develops lessons from the interests and responses of pupils and not necessarily from a previously determined plan of how enquiry should proceed.*

Are you an enquiry teacher? This book also contains a questionnaire to help you find out!

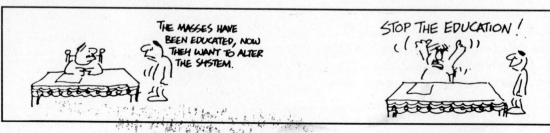

Bilingual learners

Group work has much to offer all children in their development of language. The quotations below come from a brainstorm about why group work can be of particular value to bilingual learners.

In planning group work for bilingual children, you will need to ensure that they have the opportunity to develop their command of the languages they speak, write and understand. These opportunities may need to be structured carefully, or they may arise naturally. You may need to set up groups in which all members speak a common language and can communicate using language as they wish. Afterwards, encourage them to reflect on how they used language in their groups.

All children need to feel confident about what they are doing in a group and what is expected; bilingual learners may welcome visual support which offers them a firmer grasp of the activity.

Some children may also be able to write as well as speak their language. In activities which involve writing, they could write dual texts or select one script to write in.

When children's languages are valued and become part of the fabric of the classroom, this can often lead to more direct work about languages themselves and the specific skills and knowledge which bilingual or multilingual speakers have. *The languages book*† has some useful suggestions for this kind of work.

It is worth pointing out that most people in the world speak at least two languages!

Status is given to languages other than English.

As language is being used for real communication, both monolingual and bilingual students will learn more effectively.

Bilingual children will be able to develop their language without feeling inhibited.

It offers a framework for bilingual children to really value their language skills.

Working in a peer group ensures that everyday language is used.

It gives bilingual children an opportunity to talk in their own language.

They have plenty to teach their monolingual peers.

The intellectual and cognitive development of bilingual learners is aided.

It increases language awareness.

A greater degree of participation gives more chance for language development.

In groups where teachers don't intervene, the children may be much more able to draw on their own experience.

The absence of an authority figure may encourage experimentation in expression and therefore confidence.

Bilingual learner's skills in interpreting from one language to another are valued and used.

Bilingual children are involved in the mainstream curriculum, not withdrawn for special attention.

Planning group work

If you plan to introduce some of these approaches, things will not change automatically overnight! The next few pages give practical suggestions which should ease you and your class into new ways of working.

- *'I'm sure things will get out of control.'*
- *'What about all the noise?'*
- *'I haven't got enough resources to go around.'*
- *'My children could never work in groups, they never listen to each other.'*
- *'Many of my class are bilingual, how do I make the most of this?'*

These are some common concerns which many teachers have voiced when group work is discussed. To rush into less directed group activities with a class who are used to quiet individual work may not be a wise move. However, by gradually helping children to build up skills in group work and by using appropriate techniques many of the potential problems can be minimised.

On a practical level, the way the classroom is organised can enhance or hinder collaboration. Look at the layout of the desks and other classroom furniture, does this vary in the school day or year? Further things to think about can be found in the checklist on page 22.

Staff development

For a staff team who are planning to introduce active learning methods into their classrooms, a useful starting point is to try out a similar activity in each class and then share how it went, encouraging each other with practical ideas and commiserating over the difficulties! It is best to start with a simple activity which is appropriate to different age groups. Ideas for structuring this inservice can be found in *A sense of school* [4].

When you have done some initial work in the classroom, you could use the photographs in *Behind the scenes*[5] to help reflect on the process. These photographs show a range of primary school situations, classrooms, corridors, dinnertime, children working together, isolated children etc. In groups, look at the photographs one at a time and sort them into three piles:

> *those which enhance co-operative group work;*
> *those which limit co-operative group work;*
> *those which are not relevant to the discussion.*

This really focuses the mind on what factors are necessary in the classroom or school to create an ethos which encourages children to work together. It may also highlight for your school where you need to make changes or develop what you are already doing.

Evaluating group work

It is valuable for children to reflect on how the work in the group went. This will help them to build up an awareness of what makes a group work well and a sensitivity to their peers. From time to time it is useful to get groups or pairs to discuss questions such as these suggested by Jane Sprackling [1]:

1. What did you enjoy about the task? How do you know that you enjoyed it?
2. Is there something that you did not like?
3. Did you work well as a team?
4. Did you know what the result was going to be?
5. Has it made you want to take things a step further?
6. Who asked the most questions?
7. Is there anyone who did not contribute much by speaking?
8. How could you help that person to take a more active part?
9. Are you pleased with the end result?
10. What ways of recording did you use?
11. Can you think of any other ways that you could have used?
12. Do you think that anyone was unkind or unfair to others in the group?
13. Did you all listen to each other's ideas?
14. How did you start the activity? Can you think of a different way of starting?
15. Can you think of something good or complimentary to say about all the members of the group?
16. Did you run out of time, or did you have too much time? Why do you think this was?
17. What do you think is the most important thing that you have learnt from this activity?

Take photographs as the children are working and use these afterwards to discuss how they felt about the processes of the group.

As children are working, look for signs which indicate something about the quality of co-operation e.g. body language, eye contact, touching negotiating, sharing materials etc. Brainstorm your own list of signs which you feel indicate co-operation is taking place. A further exploration of issues of shared learning can be found in *Shared learning*†.

Things to think about.....

Who should be in a group?

1. Self-selecting

If groups are self selecting this will probably be on the basis of friendship. If the children have made choices about who they work with they may be more committed to that group and therefore put more of themselves into the task. Teachers with 'isolated' children in their class may have to be more wary of this approach.

2. At random

Groups can be selected at random by counting off numbers or just by dividing up the children where they are sitting. Teachers can also use an activity which involves group forming; for instance each child could be given a photograph and has to find three others who have a photograph which connects with hers. The connections may be very loose but in the end children will have formed groups of four. The photographs can themselves be an introduction to the main group activity.

3. Selected by the teacher

- *Do you want a spread of ability in the group?*
- *Is there a particular skill which one child in the group should have? [for instance, translating for a bilingual child]*
- *If you have a group of confident children in the class, do you want to split them up or keep them together?*
- *Do you want a mix of boys and girls in a group? Are there advantages of single sex/mixed groups?*
- *How long do you want the group to work together - one session, one week, half a term? Is continuity important or do you want the children to work with as many of the class as possible?*
- *Do you want to use group work as an opportunity for encouraging children who share a home language to work together using that language?*

What size?

It is often useful to start work in pairs. Children are most likely to participate in twos as they are either talking or listening. Those who are less confident may find it easier to be fluent in a pair first of all. Even with a class who are experienced in working in groups, pair work is often a good starter for any activity. After working together, pairs can meet to form fours. Sixes are probably the largest size groups to work in normally, to allow effective participation.

Ground rules

It is useful to establish ground rules with groups before they begin, for instance that only one person can talk at once. It would also be useful to discuss ways of dealing with obvious conflict in a group.

Control

If children have a clear idea of the task they have to do and if they begin by working in pairs or with friends there are less likely to be problems of control. If behavioural problems occur, discuss with the children how these could be resolved.

Roles

It may help children to have a specific role in the group task e.g. recording comments or making sure everyone says something if they want to.

Tasks

The task the children are working on needs to be clearly defined for them. This will probably work best if they have to produce some concrete feedback e.g. a poster, a role play, an arrangement of slips of paper etc. When you introduce group work, ensure that the tasks are such that the children have to co-operate to complete them.

Recording

Sometimes it is appropriate to record the outcome of the discussion. To avoid one child always writing for the group, get them to organise their own rota, or use tapes to record ideas, share the writing between the whole group, ensuring that they all agree with what is written.

The process of the group

Children can reflect on how their group is working. A feedback session could not only include talk about the content of the discussion but also feeling about the process of the group [see opposite page].

Lack of resources

Teachers often avoid group work because they feel that more resources are needed. Newspapers, magazines, parents, children etc. can all be valuable resources for group work. Schools can review existing resources and centralise them. A review of existing resources can help you decide on what resources every classroom needs to deliver the curriculum, and which ones might effectively be centralised and stored.

Activities for skills in group work

These activities are useful for building up skills which contribute to the smooth running of a group. Some can be used regularly with a class, others can be incorporated into group activities.

THE FRIENDLY CLASSROOM FOR A SMALL PLANET

WINNERS ALL

co-operative games for all ages

The circle

To begin and end an activity it is useful to sit the whole class in a circle. This is a physical way of emphasising the importance of everyone in the group. It also can encourage participation. Go round the circle and ask each child to contribute something if they would like, but making sure that they have an option to pass.

At the beginning of a lesson it could be a warm up activity introducing the subject of the lesson; at the end it could be a comment on the activity. This helps to gain a sense of being part of a class not just a small group.

Co-operation activities

If children are going to work together in groups they need to be able to co-operate. Competition is often emphasised in primary schools to the exclusion of co-operative learning and playing. Here are a few starting points for co-operative group work.

Co-operative spelling
Can children spell words with letters made by bodies? Small groups can spell a word and the rest of the class guess. It may be easier to lie flat on the floor to do this. What is the longest word you can spell? How many children can you involve in one word?

Musical laps
This is a non-competitive form of musical chairs. The children form a circle close together and hold the waist of the person in front. When the music starts everyone walks slowly forward, when it stops everyone sits on the lap behind. If you are co-operating the circle will stay up and everyone will have a lap to sit on - if not then everyone will end up on the floor!

Another variation of musical chairs is to play with chairs as normal but while the chairs are gradually removed the children stay in and eventually have to sit on one chair.

Painting
Painting is usually an individualised activity. How about giving four children one sheet of paper and ask them to paint - the park, the school etc?

Affirmation activities

It is very difficult for children to contribute with confidence to a group or class if they have a low self image, therefore it is important to enable children to develop self confidence. Affirmation activities can help build up a positive self image. They involve not only the teacher in affirming children, but also children affirming each other.

One good thing.......
Everyone sits in a circle, ask each child to make one positive comment about the child on their left. Encourage comments about the person rather than about superficialities like their clothes, comments like 'One good thing about Fiona is that she helps me with my maths'.

Stocking fillers
Everyone in the groups hangs up a sock with their name on it. Ask each child to write their name on top of five slips of paper. These all go into a hat and everyone draws out five slips of paper and writes one positive thing about the person named. These papers are put in the socks so each person will have five positive statements about themselves.

Pairs - self affirmation
In pairs, one person has to talk for about two minutes about the positive things about himself/herself, the other listens. Then swap over. How did you find this activity? [Adults find it extremely difficult!]

Children often find it quite difficult to listen to other members of a group, and respond to what they are saying. Listening skills are essential to group work, these activities may help.

Whispers

Sit in a circle, one person makes up a sentence and whispers it to the person on one side. This whisper is passed around the circle. What does the last person hear? Is it distorted? If it is, you can use this to think about what helps people to hear what is said.

Try the activity again and ask the children to concentrate on communicating clearly. This time if they do not hear clearly they can check with the speaker what is said.

Magic microphone

This activity can help groups listen to one person at a time. Each group has a 'magic microphone' [this can be a pen, a paint brush, a shell etc.] - only the child with the 'magic microphone' is allowed to speak. After s/he has spoken, s/he looks for signs of who wants to speak next and passes them the magic microphone.

Storytelling

Groups of children make up a story together. One child with a magic microphone starts and the others have to listen to what s/he says. After about a minute or so s/he passes the magic microphone to another who continues the story.

Paraphrasing

This can be done in small groups or in a class. The aim is not to catch people out but to think about how carefully we listen. Choose a subject which is relevant to the group e.g. playtime. Ask the first child to talk for a very short time on playtime - the second child then has to paraphrase [express the main points about] what was said. To do this the second child has to listen very carefully. The two can then swap roles.

Over 300 co-operative games for children and adults

Mildred Masheder

A number of publications suggest activities such as those described opposite. These are a few of the ones we have found most useful.

Self esteem: a classroom affair, Volumes 1 and 2, Michele and Craig Borba, Harper and Row [1982].

Let's co-operate - activities and ideas for parents and teachers of young children for peaceful conflict solving, Mildred Masheder, Peace Education Project [1986].

Let's play together - over 300 co-operative games for children and adults, Mildred Masheder, Greenprint [1989].

Co-operating for a change, Newcastle upon Tyne LEA [1987].

The co-operative sports and games book - challenge without competition, by Terry Orlick, Writers and Readers [1978].

Winners all, co-operative games for all ages, Pax Christi, London [1980].

The friendly classroom for a small planet, ed Priscilla Prutzmann, New Society Publishers [1988].

Discussion

When children have discussed ideas together in small groups, it is valuable to share them with the whole class. These suggestions are aimed at those organising and facilitating class discussion.

With the whole class

Class discussion is important for bringing together children's ideas and encouraging others to challenge them. Unless a class discussion is managed carefully, it may only benefit the most fluent children and those with the broadest attention span. Class discussion may be doing different things, such as:

- sharing information and ideas e.g. before a piece of creative writing;
- feeding back from a group work activity;
- looking at an issue e.g. discussing the validity of a school rule;
- making a decision e.g. where should we go for the class visit;
- planning how to do something e.g. how to split up the work for a class assembly.

Feeding back

It is difficult for some children to report to the whole class. This can be eased if they have something 'concrete' to refer to, e.g. a group poster. Other useful techniques for channelling feedback are:

- *share one important point from your discussion;*
- *share one area of disagreement in the group;*
- *from a ranking* or organising activity share the top and bottom cards of the diamond;*
- *dramatise one aspect of your discussion;*
- *share one question from the group.*

The feedback session could also involve some reflection on the processes of the groups [see page 30].

Highlights

You may want to highlight certain points in a final discussion; a useful technique is to jot a few ideas down before the lesson which can form a 'mental checklist'. Even if you do not refer to the list in the lesson, the process of thinking beforehand helps.

Your role

In each situation it is important for the teacher to be aware of the role she is taking in the discussion. Jean Rudduck in her book *Learning to teach through discussion*[6] takes five role models, outlined here briefly, which are commonly used by teachers in discussions. In any one lesson you may take on more than one role. It is often useful to clarify what that role is and to be aware of its limitations. It may be helpful to read through the list and ask yourself:

- *Which role model you identify with most closely.*
- *Which you would like to identify with most closely.*
- *How you might increase the children's responsibility for the discussion.*

Roles

Instructor - giving background information at appropriate points, and conducting the discussion.
Limitations: the children may become dependent on the teacher for the input and may be over influenced by what the teacher says.

Participant - taking part in the discussion on the same basis as the children.
Limitations: the children may give more weight to the teacher's view or opinion without being critical of it.

Devil's advocate - challenging the group with new angles on the subject, often offering different arguments to widen the debate.
Limitations: the role can show the teacher's cleverness in being able to represent different viewpoints - it can create dependency on the teacher for new ideas.

Neutral chairperson - encouraging independent thinking in the group by expressing no personal opinion in the discussion, throwing back ideas and questions raised by the group for them to discuss.
Limitations: there may be areas in which the teacher feels it necessary to express an opinion.

Consultant - withdrawing from the discussion so that the children organise the discussion themselves and use the teacher as someone to consult.
Limitations: the role could be seen as an opting out of managing a difficult group, or it could imply that the teacher is full of wisdom to be tapped.

The next thirteen pages outline some useful learning approaches which can be adapted for all kinds of themes. They are set out for easy reference in the same format. These activities are referred to in the rest of the text by an asterisk *.

STARTING POINTS

These activities are designed to find out what the children already know and what they want to find out.

They are useful techniques for:
- **introducing a new theme;**
- **finding out what is already known and what assumptions are made about a particular theme;**
- **enabling children to take some responsiblity for the direction of their work;**
- **sharing information and assumptions.**

What do you know? What do you want to know?
Give each pair or group a sheet of paper drawn in two columns, like the one shown here. Ask them to write everything they know about the theme on the left hand side. These ideas can be shared with the class.

In the right hand column, ask them to write a list of questions which they would like to find out more about, as part of this theme. Some questions will be able to be answered straight away by other members of the class, others will need further research.

A third stage involves identifying how these questions might be answered. The children could try doing this themselves, or you could give them particular types of sources, e.g. people, books, television, maps etc. which might help them clarify their ideas.

Brainstorming, as shown on the next page, is an ideal starter activity.

True or false?
When introducing a new theme you will need to find out what the children already know. Take a series of statements about the subject, some of which are true, others of which are false. Ask groups to sort them into two piles, true or false.

If you are taking an issue centred approach, ask them to sort statements about different points of view.

What we know...	What we would like to know...

BRAINSTORMING

Brainstorming involves expressing a wide variety of ideas without comment.

It is a useful technique for:
- **finding out what is already known and what assumptions are made about a particular theme;**
- **problem solving;**
- **giving participants an opportunity to identify what they already know or think and share that in a co-operative atmosphere;**
- **bringing a wide range of views to a situation.**

Each group will need a felt tipped pen and a sheet of sugar paper.

Procedure

Brainstorming is ideal for group work, although as an introduction you may want to try it out with the whole class. Appoint a scribe to write down everything that is said. Take a subject, theme or question and get everyone to call out as many ideas as they can think of about it. The quantity of ideas is more important than the quality. Encourage far fetched ideas! Bilingual children may like to brainstorm with others who speak the same language.

There should be no discussion at this point, this is important because it allows a wide response; people often feel less inhibited about contributing if they know their ideas are not going to be criticised. The scribe can add ideas as well. The children may want to rotate the role of scribe; it is worth remembering that sometimes the person who holds the pen also holds the power in the group. It is best to limit this activity to five or ten minutes to concentrate thinking time.

Follow up

You will need to do something with all the ideas which have come up. Get groups to organise their ideas, e.g.by linking similar ones together or by underlining the ten most surprising ideas. For a more thorough follow up, each comment could be discussed individually. To explore ideas in greater detail, you could get the class to focus in on the more promising ideas arising from the brainstorm.

At a workshop, teachers brainstormed what concerned them about multicultural/anti-racist education. As a way of organising their ideas constructively, so they were not left feeling overwhelmed by problems, they placed coloured dots next to each comment as follows:

- *a red dot for something I can respond to as an individual;*
- *a green dot for something my school can respond to;*
- *a blue dot for something the L.E.A. can respond to;*
- *a yellow dot for something that cannot be changed.*

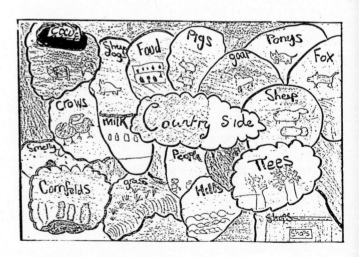

A group of children from Birmingham did some work on the differences between life in the city and in the countryside. They brainstormed their ideas and then drew these posters.

SORTING ACTIVITIES

Sorting activities involve making decisions about how to group a variety of statements, objects, pictures etc.

They are useful techniques for:
- encouraging children to co-operate in making choices;
- discussing a range of points of view and therefore very valuable for issue centred learning;
- showing the children that items can be sorted into many different sub sets;
- developing discussion skills such as criticising, judging, defending, arguing, listening, comparing and contrasting.

Each group will need a set of objects, photographs, pictures, sentences, points of view, statements etc.

Procedure

Sorting is a familar activity to those who work with young children. It holds great potential for maths, science and issue centred work. There are many variations on the same theme. The basis of the activity lies in organising the items into two or more groups. These groupings can be suggested by the teacher or the children can define their own. Because the focus is on talk, bilingual children may value this opportunity to work together.

Objects

Give the children a set of objects. They could include objects from different parts of the world, from the past and present, or objects which at first seem to have no obvious connection to each other. These are some examples of ones you could use:

- fresh food, such as fruits and vegetables, including those grown in other parts of the world;
- household items from different parts of the world;
- toys;
- a shopping basket of food;
- a bag of clothes with labels of countries of manufacture.

An initial activity might be to ask the children to sort them into two groups. When they have done this, you could ask them to try and sort them into another two groups. This may be much more difficult as they will have to dismantle the first sets and think up different groupings.

Another way of using the objects would be to first ask the children to sort them into three sets. This is usually more challenging that sorting into two as they cannot use opposites such as old and new or large and small as criteria. It is likely to create much more imaginative discussion.

Statements

When developing a theme around an issue, it is important that the children are aware that people hold different points of view around the issue in question. Give the children a set of statements showing various viewpoints and ask them to sort them into those they agree with and those they disagree with.

When they have sorted and discussed them, the children could add their own. Alternatively, in pairs, one could argue in favour and the other against a particular statement.

Venn diagrams

These are a valuable structure for sorting ideas and items. The one below can be used when you are looking at the future dimensions of an issue. If you are looking at the dangers of acid rain, you could give the children statements about what might happen and ask them to sort them into:

- *what is likely to happen*
- *what could happen*
- *not sure?*

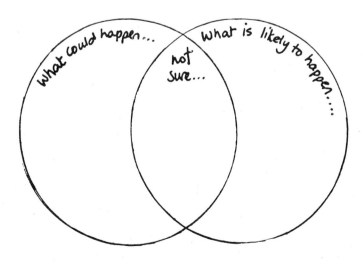

RANKING

Ranking involves prioritising pictures, photographs or statements.

It is a useful technique for:
- **encouraging people to co-operate in making choices;**
- **thinking about priorities;**
- **developing discussion skills such as criticising, judging, defending, arguing, listening, comparing and contrasting.**

Each group will need nine 'cards'; these might consist of photographs, pictures, sentences, anecdotes, quotations, adverts, cartoons etc.

Procedure

This technique works best with small groups, ideally of four or five. The aim of the activity is to arrange the cards in a diamond pattern, ordering them carefully so that the whole group agrees with the arrangement. The card selected as most important is placed at the top of the diamond, the least important at the base and the others between.

Ask the group to look at each card in turn and debate where it should be placed in the diamond. It is important to look at and discuss each card separately, if the final decision is to be a considered one. This will mean discussing choices in detail. The mechanics of the making of the diamond encourages discussion, although the discussion itself is the most important part of this activity. Bilingual children may value the opportunity to operate in common language groups, especially if the stimulus is visual.

Groups could feedback their first and last choices and discuss why they were chosen. The process of group discussion could also be talked about. Did the group come to the same choice easily? Was everyone involved equally, or did one person dominate? Were there any important points raised in the small group to share with the whole group?

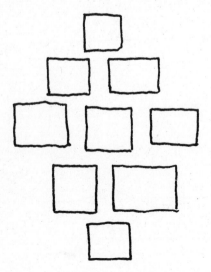

Clothes

'I wanted the class to think about their attitudes to clothes as this was becoming a divisive issue among some of the children. They were divided into groups of four and each group was given nine slips of paper with comments on about clothes. I explained to them that I wanted them to organise the slips into a diamond putting at the top of the diamond the comment they agreed with most, and the one at the base that they agreed with least. This stimulated a lively discussion in the group about clothes and was a good starting point for exploring attitudes to dress'.

Comments on clothes

Children should not wear earrings and bangles in school.

I always want to choose my own clothes; my mum chooses boring clothes.

It does not matter what you wear, what is important is what kind of person you are.

Girls should not be allowed to wear trousers in school.

Uniforms always look very smart.

I only like people who wear fashionable clothes.

It's silly to follow fashion, as soon as you buy something it's out of date.

Expensive clothes are always nicer than cheap ones.

Clothes should last for a long time and keep you warm, that's all that matters.

TIMELINES

A timeline is created by marking a set of events on a line in chronological order.

It is a useful technique for:
- **thinking about how things progress and change;**
- **sequencing events;**
- **recalling past experiences and sharing them with others;**
- **building up empathy with other people;**
- **thinking about possible future events.**

Pens, crayons, felt tipped pens and a sheet of paper or strip of card per person.

Procedure

Although this is essentially an individual activity because each child is creating a personal timeline, it is best done in a co-operative atmosphere. Children should sit in groups and be encouraged to talk to each other as they are writing and drawing, using each others ideas of presentation if they wish.

Give each child a sheet of paper with a line down the centre of it to form the basis of the timeline. Ask everyone to think about the main events which have happened to them in their lives and record them briefly in order on this line. At the left hand end might be birth or some other defined time like starting school; at the right hand end could be today. They should be encouraged to illustrate their timelines as colourfully as possible. It may also help to give some notion of scale although this is not always necessary. In groups, children could explain their timelines to each other and then some central points could be shared with the whole class.

'My class found it quite difficult to get events in their lives in the right order; they could not remember which came first. We got over this by writing the events and illustrating them on small slips of paper and then putting them in the right order and sticking them on to the timelines. This in itself created quite a lot of discussion.'

Timelines of other people

This activity is to encourage empathy with others. Have a selection of photographs of children and adults from different backgrounds. The faces on page 101 would be ideal.

Give pairs or small groups one photograph and ask them to build a timeline of changes for that person. If they have a picture of a child ask them to do a timeline from childhood to adulthood - if they have a picture of an adult ask them to work backwards to childhood.

Timelines can be extended into the future; projections could be made about what might happen in 10, 15 or 20 years time.

'The class of infants had not done anything like this before so I thought I would introduce a timeline of what went on in school in the morning. We discussed all the different events that went on; I found this was essential before we actually put pen to paper. Then I gave each child a long strip of paper and some wax crayons and they drew pictures to illustrate the different events. These who could, also wrote comments. When we discussed them afterwards I found that they were able to move away from concrete ideas to abstract ones.'

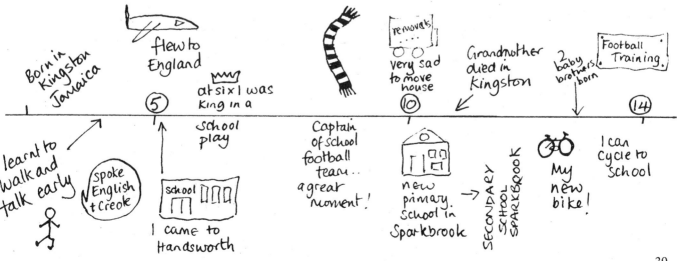

39

MENTAL MAPS

Drawing a mental map involves expressing how you see a place in the form of a drawing.

It is a useful technique for:
- **exploring feelings and attitudes about a place or an issue;**
- **clarifying thoughts and ideas by having to express them in pictorial form;**
- **sharing ideas with other children;**
- **stimulating discussion about images and attitudes.**

Each person will need a sheet of paper and something to draw with - felt tipped pens or crayons give more variety than pencils but anything can be used.

Procedure

It is important to emphasise that producing a 'mental map' is not like producing an ordinary street map or world map. The idea of this activity is to draw something which expresses how you feel about the subject in question. It may be easier to begin this work by looking at other people's mental maps as a stimulus for discussion. It also may be helpful to pick a subject for which there are no 'geographical' maps, such as the dining room or your journey to school.

Mental maps reflect how each individual sees something, so they need to be produced by each child on his/her own. If children sit in groups they may be interested in seeing how others' maps develop, but it should be stressed that there are not 'right' and 'wrong' maps - all are equally valid as they represent the children's ideas. This may serve to give confidence to children whose 'map' is perhaps different.

A good starter might be to draw a 'mental' map of something familiar like the classroom. If the children are sitting in the classroom at the time this could influence their mental picture so it is best to take them to another part of the school. Ask the children to draw from memory how they see their classroom, including important areas. For instance, a painting on the wall might be important to one child whereas the clock and the pile of books in the corner may be important to another.

When the children have finished their drawings, ask them to get into pairs and compare their pictures looking especially for similarities and differences. This is important because each child is translating his/her pictures into words, thus expressing attitudes in words.

Follow up

The class could discuss why they drew different pictures or why certain items might have figured on most pictures. What do the pictures tell you about the person who drew them? What attitudes were brought out by the pictures? Were there any surprising things said in the groups or drawn in the pictures?

Ask the children to imagine a visitor who knew nothing about the class was coming to find out about them and their classroom. The only evidence he has is the drawings. In groups ask the children to imagine what he might deduce.

Imagine you have just met a friendly visitor from outer space who has never been to earth before. You are the very first human being he meets and he wants to know about planet earth. He does not understand your language, so you have to draw a picture for him. Draw a picture which shows the main things happening in the world at the moment.

This mental map shows what one woman remembered of her primary education; the girls used to do dancing while the boys were sent out for football.

ROLE PLAY

Role play is a technique which allows people to identify with others and discover new ways of understanding.

It is a useful technique for:
- **finding solutions to a conflict/problem;**
- **finding out what it is like to be in someone else's shoes;**
- **building up confidence;**
- **developing communication and listening skills;**
- **preparing for unknown situations such as meeting new people.**

Materials are not usually needed, although photographs, stories, newspaper cuttings, cartoons, poems etc. could all be used as a stimulus to role play.

Procedure

Choose a specific situation which you want to role play. Often this will be a spontaneous response to something that has happened in the classroom. Decide how many people are involved in this incident and the roles of those involved. Divide children into appropriate groups. Bilingual children may want to role play with their friends who speak the same language. Set the scene of the situation by giving details such as time, place, recent events or presenting a problem.

A few valuable minutes can be spent before the role play actually begins, looking at the different characters, each person thinking about their character and getting into role. Let the role play work itself through to a natural conclusion. It may be necessary to put a time limit on the groups, as some groups will never come to a satisfactory conclusion.

Follow up

The debriefing part of the role play is an integral part of the activity. Various points might be raised such as what conclusions groups came to, what people in the groups felt at various points, what they think they learnt.

Role reversal

To help people look at different sides of the same situation, the role play could be repeated but with the roles switched. What new insights do you gain from this? Has a different solution been reached? How did the characters feel in the other role?

Freeze

At some point during a role play the teacher could call 'freeze' and the action stops. This break in the role play could be used to ask a question about what characters are feeling or could be used for them to discuss what is going on.

Observer

It helps in the debriefing if someone has acted as the observer for a group and can give a more objective view of what has gone on.

The accident

'As an introduction to some work on bias, we wanted to help children understand that different people hold different points of view. We took a situation of an accident which involved a police officer, parent, child, onlooker and driver. The children were put into groups of five, each chose their role and thought about it. They were told that they were going to role play an accident where the child would be run over by a vehicle. We told them that they were to concentrate on their own role and how they saw the accident. Some of the accidents were pretty gruesome and one girl in particular really got into the role of a distraught mother! After we had talked about the accidents, we talked about the different points of view which the people hold. Each child then wrote a newspaper account form their particular standpoint. Some found this quite difficult and ended up writing a general description of the accident; others managed to get into the role and describe what went on through their own eyes.'

USING PHOTOGRAPHS

The next four pages suggest activities for developing a critical awareness of photographs.

Visual images have always been a popular teaching resource in the primary school, they focus children's attention and act as a stimulus for talk. They bring in wider experiences of people and places outside the children's immediate surroundings; they can also acknowledge and reflect the children's own experience.

As resources, photographs often stand on their own, uncriticised, yet every photograph is a selection of some kind, a selection by the photographer, the publisher and the person using it. As well as using photographs as illustrations, we need to help children build up skills in 'reading' photographs; visual literacy is as important as print literacy. Children need to understand that the messages which photographs give are influenced by the attitudes and perceptions of the viewer.

The national curriculum for English indicates the importance of media education when it says:
'Children can be encouraged to think of watching television or films, or looking at pictures as a kind of 'reading'. By looking closely at visual images and discussing exactly what they can see, children can begin to see how most still and moving images are organised on purpose, and how visual conventions and symbols are used.' [7]

The *Images* section takes these ideas a great deal further, as does *Get the picture! developing visual literacy in the infant classroom* [8].

The photo activities can be used with any photographs, such as magazines, newspapers, postcards etc. See page 82 for ideas. We have found the published photopacks on page 88 are particularly useful resources.

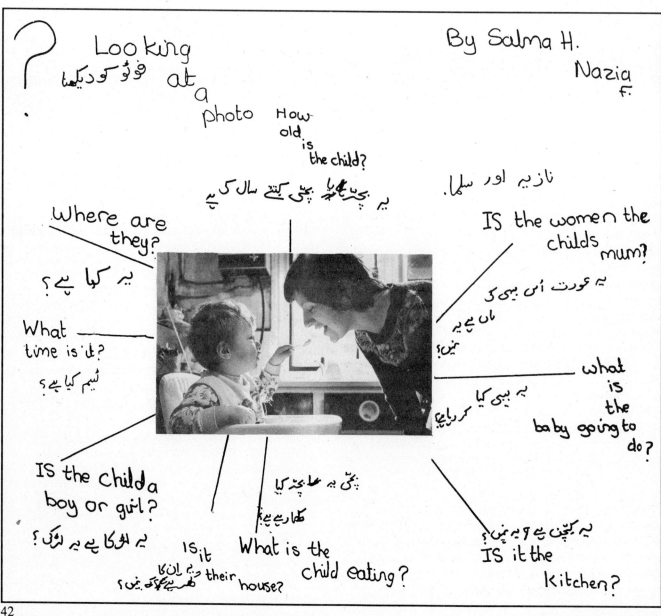

42

1. OBSERVATION

These activities are designed to help children build up skills in observation of detail.

These activities are useful for:
- studying photographs in detail and observing what is happening in them;
- helping children find their own language for referring to photographs;
- building up confidence in looking at, and talking about, photographs.

Photographs etc.

Kim's game

This traditional party game can be used to encourage close observation. Lay out a set of photographs on a table top and ask the children to look at them for one minute. Then all but one close their eyes and the person with their eyes open turns over one photograph. Which photograph has been turned? The one who guesses correctly can turn over next time. The whole set of photographs might be removed and the children try and remember what the set consisted of.

Twenty questions

With a set of photographs on display, a child selects one but does not reveal her choice to the others. By asking twenty questions the group or class has to identify the correct picture. The only answers that can be given are 'yes' and 'no'.

Connecting photographs

Give a group of children two photographs and ask them to make as many connections as they can between the two pictures. They will have to observe closely in order to make connections.

Describing a photograph

Children work in pairs and one of the pair is given a photograph. She has to describe that photograph in detail to her partner without letting her partner see it. The partner could draw the photograph from the description and then compare it to the original. How is it different? What was omitted from the description? What was made up? The illustration opposite was drawn by a seven year old in response to a friend's description of a photo.

Questioning a photograph

Having developed observation skills, it is important to build on these by questioning what you observe, for instance by questioning a photograph. It is probably best demonstrated first by the teacher with the whole class.

Give a photograph placed in the centre of a large sheet of paper to each group. Ask them to write as many different questions as they can think of about the photograph. These should be written on the large sheet of paper with arrows going to the appropriate edge of the photograph. Children who can write in more than one script could do a dual language brainstorm, as shown opposite. When they have finished, they could

categorise them into different types of questions:

- *those which require further information from books or other sources;*
- *those which are easily answered;*
- *those which have no defined answer, but which lead to wider debate about the issues raised in the picture.*

Questions also highlight attitudes and assumptions and this again could be a good discussion starter. It is important that children understand that there are not clear cut answers to a lot of questions and that many answers are based on opinion, although they might sound factual.

Fact and opinion

It might be useful at this stage to do some work differentiating between fact and opinion. Give each group a photograph with a series of statements about it. Some of them should be factual, e.g. the woman's hair is curly; others should reflect opinions, e.g. it's the most beautiful tree in the forest. Ask the children to sort them into two piles, fact and opinion.

2. LABELLING

Labelling activities involve choosing words to describe a person or situation.

These activities are useful for:
- **raising awareness that people have preconceived ideas or prejudices;**
- **showing that first impressions and superficial judgements are not necessarily right;**
- **bringing into the open, images and stereotypes held by the group.**

Photographs etc. blutac, slips of paper.

Procedure

Display a set of numbered photographs and ask the children to brainstorm as many adjectives as they can about those pictures. Both 'negative' and 'positive' adjectives should be included. These adjectives can be written on the board for all to see. It is better to have more adjectives than photographs. Alternatively, you could begin with a list of adjectives.

Give each pair a sheet of paper with the numbers of the photographs on and ask them to record next to the number the adjective or adjectives which they think most appropriate. A limit could be set on the number of adjectives which can be used per photograph, or the number of times an adjective can be used. Pairs could form groups of four and discuss their choices.

Follow up

To stimulate a discussion, each photograph could be looked at in turn and the groups could share the adjectives they used for that picture. Was there a tendency to use the same words or different words on a photograph? Did some photographs only have negative words? Does anyone disagree with the labels given?

Imagine someone else is writing labels, for instance parents or teachers. Would they be different?

Captions

This activity is useful in bringing out different perceptions of a picture. Display about a dozen photographs, ask each pair to choose a photograph from the selection. It does not matter if more than one pair chooses the same photograph. Ask each pair to write a list of short captions for that photograph. Those who can write in a language other than English, may like to add multilingual captions.

It might be useful beforehand to get the children to draw bubbles coming from the mouths of the people in the photograph and imagine what they are saying. This can help give ideas for captions.

What is a family? [9]

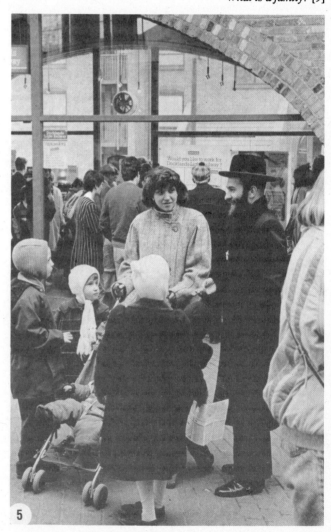

5

Each pair then has to select out of this list one caption which they think is most appropriate. It can then be written on a strip of paper and attached to the photograph on display. Did they see different things in the same picture? Which caption and picture match the best? What do you think the person who wrote this caption was thinking?

A variation of this is to give the group a set of headlines and ask the children to attach them to a set of photographs.

3. SELECTION

These activities involve making choices about certain photographs.

These activities are useful for:
- **individuals making their own personal choices and justifying them;**
- **developing debating and discussion skills;**
- **raising issues from photographs;**
- **revealing people's perceptions and challenging them.**

Photographs etc. stickers.

Personal selection

This is a good activity for introducing a photopack as a whole. The photographs are displayed on the wall or on a desk top and each child is given three coloured stickers [red] or slips of paper. They are asked to look carefully at the whole set of photographs and then choose three. The criteria for selection should be kept as simple as possible, for instance:

- *choose the pictures which appeal to you;*
- *choose the pictures which surprise you;*
- *choose the pictures which annoy you.*

A sticker should be put on/by the photographs selected. This could lead into a discussion about why certain choices were made.

This activity can be developed in several ways. In the first part ask the children to write their name/initials on their stickers. Ask them to find someone who has chosen the same picture[s]. The pair can then discuss why they chose the particular picture and which others they chose.

Individuals have to find a partner and each shows the other the photographs they chose and explains their choices. The pair then have to select three photographs between them out of their original choices. They indicate their joint decision by three different coloured stickers [green]. Pairs then come together in groups of four to describe their choices to each other and then make a final choice of three, a final set of stickers [yellow] can be used. This activity is excellent for showing that we have different ideas, opinions and feelings about photographs and that one is not inherently right. A lot of justifying, defending arguments and listening has to go on in order to reach a consensus.

If this is done with younger children it can be simplified by asking them to select four photographs at each stage; this will probably mean they will choose 'two of yours and two of mine'.

When we have used the *What is a family?* [9]photopack with predominantly white group of children, we have found that they rarely choose photographs depicting families from ethnic minority groups. When this has been highlighted in discus-sions it has been useful for thinking about children's perceptions of multicultural Britain.

Stepladder

This activity, described in the *Doing things* [10] handbook is useful for making selections.

Each pupil has a piece of paper with a ladder drawn on it. The ladder has nine rungs. The teacher holds up nine photographs, one at a time. As each photograph is held up pupils have to enter a one-word or one-phrase description of it on one of the rungs of their ladder. ['Cooking', 'fishing', 'playing with soldiers', 'cleaning windows'.] The more they like the activity, or think they would like it if they tried it, the higher the rung on which they place it.

Of course, when the first photograph is held up, no-one knows what the other eight will be. Nevertheless a description of it must be placed on the ladder. Later the descriptions can be moved around; the ladder can, therefore, become very untidy.

When each pupil has completed his or her ladder, a chart can be dawn up to show the choices of the class or group as a whole. There is likely to be useful discussion as pupils explain and defend their rankings to each other.

A photograph from the *Doorways* pack [11]

4. PERCEPTIONS

Perceptions activities are designed to bring out children's underlying attitudes about a given photograph.

These activities are useful for:
- **raising issues about how we see things, and that we bring images and assumptions to every situation;**
- **recognising that people hold different points of view;**
- **highlighting personal attitudes.**

Photographs etc.

Additions

It is important to recognise that any group of photographs or pictures is a selection, whether it is a published pack or a teacher's choice. A useful activity to help children realise this, is to display a photopack and ask them to say which photographs they would add to a photopack. This will probably bring out their images and assumptions.

Cropping

Each group is presented with part of a picture, the aim is to guess the whole picture. With this information, they are to look closely at clues such as expressions on faces, body positions, background, dress etc. When they have decided on what they imagine the whole picture to be they can then contrast them with the complete picture. How did the complete picture differ from what you expected? Are there any parts of the completed picture which would have completely changed their guess? Does this activity show you anything about your stereotypes and images? The example shown here is taken from the *Working now* [12] pack.

Rumour clinic

This activity is useful for showing how easy it is to develop a misguided image from a little information, and how easy it is to embroider details which have not been given. It shows how attitudes and expectations affect what we see. It works best with a slide or a large photograph which depicts either a very active situation or one with which the children are not familiar.

Several [up to six] children leave the room and the rest look at the photograph or slide. After they have had time to take in the contents, it is removed. One of the outsiders is asked to return and the class describe what they have seen. The second outsider returns and the first describes what s/he has been told [s/he still has not seen the slide]. This process continues, bringing in one person at a time until all who left have been told of the slide.

While this is going on, the class are asked to note what has been transmitted accurately and what has become distorted. Everyone then sees the picture again and the activity concludes with a discussion about the misconceptions.

It is inevitable that in this activity the last person is not going to give an accurate description of the image. It must be made clear that this is because of the nature of the activity and the responsibility of everyone involved up to that point [including the main group], not just of the last person.

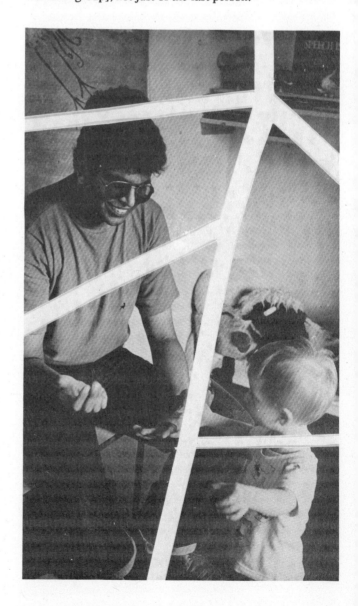

Getting out and about

These are examples of activities which take you out of the classroom and into the outside world.

These activities are useful for:
- **introducing a wide variety of stimuli to children's learning;**
- **encouraging a multi sensory approach;**
- **building observation skills;**
- **raising issues about the local environment;**
- **developing links between the school and the community.**

Various.

Most of children's formal learning relies on experiences, knowledge and resources which can be brought into the confines of the classroom. The world outside the classroom is a vastly under-used resource for direct, hands on experiential learning.

Framing it

You may not even have to go outside the school gates. Many schools are now developing a wild area or pond in the school grounds. In pairs, get children to observe what is going on in a tiny area of grass, or water or plant life. They can make their own frames by cutting out a 6cm square out of the centre of an A5 sheet of paper. Place the 'frame' on the ground and see what happens in the small area over a period of 5 or 10 minutes. How can they record what they have observed?

- *Sit silently, what can you hear?*
- *Breathe deeply, what can you smell?*
- *Can you taste anything?*

Many activities for outdoor environmental education have been developed through local environmental studies centres and through the Institute for Earth Education [for address, see page 111]. *Sunship earth* †, *Acclimatization* † and *Sharing nature with children* † suggest practical activities.

A walk round the area

Go for a walk round the local area, in groups as small as possible. The children could be looking at one specific thing e.g. the design of doors, street names etc. Traditional surveys can also be a useful trigger as long as all the attention isn't so directed to collecting data that other opportunities for discussion are lost.

A more open ended 'walk' might involve just watching the world go by. Sit on a low wall, or bench and look at what is happening. Focus this by using frames [this time with a larger viewfinder] in pairs and watching a spot for three minutes. Can they draw one image, like a photograph that has occurred on the viewfinder while they watched? What did they think was happening?

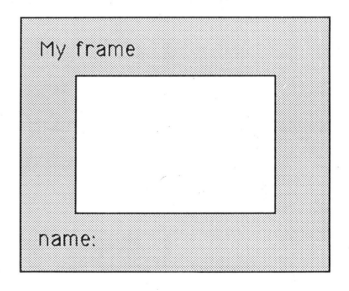

Go for a 'print walk' and note down all the different kinds of print which can be found.

School visits

A day trip, or a residential visit can offer, many opportunities for learning. What do the children expect to find/experience before they go? How does it compare to what they found out? A further exploration of this idea can be found on page 90.

The Development Education Centre has a tradition of going out and about as part of inservice. A group who were planning to visit East Africa on a study visit, prepared by going into a small community for an afternoon with the task of finding out what the development issues were for that community. The experience raised some fundamental questions about how we learn about people and places, how preconceptions and incomplete information can result in a distorted view.

Resources: Group work

Acclimatization - a sensory and conceptual approach to ecological involvement, Steve van Matre, American Camping Association 1972, available from High Borrans, Outdoor Education Centre, Windermere, Cumbria LA23 1JS.
An earth education programme to introduce young people to the natural world; this book describes some outdoor sessions in great detail. They offer a dynamic alternative to the traditional field trip type format, but can also be adapted for use in the local area.

Co-operative group work, Jane Sprackling, Manchester City Council Education Department.
A booklet written as a result of a one term secondment to look at co-operative group work in the primary classroom. Some useful ideas.

Doorways, IYSH, Ikon Productions, 1987.
An A4 photoset in black/white and colour which shows housing and homes in different parts of the world, e.g. high rise flats in London, an inside of a Columbian house, a house on stilts in the Pacific. The photos and teachers' notes give many suggestions on how you might use this resource to give a different angle to a theme on 'Homes'.

Effective questioning, Trevor Kerry, DES/MacMillan Educational, 1982.
How we ask questions often determines the answers we receive. This booklet examines the art of questioning and suggests how we can become more conscious of the questions we ask.

Getting on without the teacher, primary school pupils in co-operative groups, Colin Biott, Sunderland polytechnic, 1984.
This report argues that we need to plan strategies to raise the status of co-operation in an education system which only tends to reward private, individual attainment.

Handling classroom groups, Trevor Kerry and Margaret Sands, DES/MacMillan Educational, 1982.
This booklet suggests ways of organising group work. It discusses issues like the role of the teacher and the duration and nature of tasks. The text is filled with examples of teachers' experiences of group work to clarify the points made.

The languages book, ILEA English Centre, 1981.
An excellent teachers' handbook which suggests how to talk about written and spoken language in the classroom. Attractively laid out, it is full of teaching ideas which could be useful for anyone exploring language with children.

The learning process, Patrick Whitaker, World Studies Journal Vol. 5. No. 2, 1984.
An edition of the World Studies Journal about 'person centred' teaching Suggestions for organising group work, looking into attitudes, organising plenary sessions are included. Each section is clearly set out with suggestions for classroom practice, questions for teachers to reflect on and book references for further ideas.

Learning together, global education 4-7, Susan Fountain, Stanley Thornes/WWF, 1990.
A practical teachers' handbook that shows how to develop the essential skills of self esteem, communication and co-operation. It provides masses of classroom activities and games and shows how to integrate them into the core national curriculum.

Shared learning - an active learning approach to the infant curriculum, Cathy de Vesey, DEC, 1990.
A new book for infants teachers which describes some of the work involved in a shared learning project. Examples are given across the curriculum of how young children can collaborate. Practical ideas are suggested for setting up, observing and evaluating the quality of children's shared learning experiences.

Sharing nature with children, Joseph Bharat Cornell, Exley publications, 1979.
An imaginative handbook for parents, play leaders and teachers who seek to inspire children's imagination about the world outdoors. The games it suggests are simple and fun. They build on children's natural affinity with nature and teach them to respect it rather than exploit it.

Sunship earth - an earth education program getting to know your place in space, Steve van Matre, American Camping Association, 1979/89. Available from: High Borrans, see above.
An environmental education programme to help children understand how their world functions, using all their senses. The activities build both on concepts such as the water cycle and also engage children's feelings in relationship to their surroundings. Earth education has much to teach us about a multisensory approach.

What is a country?

Beyond nationalism
[for K. J. Ratnam]
From distances shorter
than the moon
continents are a blur
you cannot tell
one country from another.

Seen from the stars
how absurd we seem
with our border wars
- petty squabbles
over neighbours' fences

We are so small
no more than neutrons
on a speck of dust
floating in the galaxy;
still we're asked
to thump our chest
trumpet our nationality.

Cecil Rajendra, *taken from Dove on fire [1].*

This theme is an extended simulation designed to help children to explore what they already know about countries and to develop their understanding of ways in which countries are interdependent yet have their own identities. The approach focuses on children discovering what countries have in common. It offers an opportunity to explore the concept of place in general terms, and then to look at more specific issues about interdependence. The latter part of the theme gives plenty of scope for looking at particular issues such as food, tourism, trading etc. Having established some context for children's learning, you could take the work further by looking at one country in particular.

In the national curriculum
What is a country? lends itself to a geography focus, but within that context there is scope for developing other concepts and ideas. The potential for English and history are also highlighted in the theme; alternatively you might choose to focus on design and technology, personal and social education or RE. The web on page 53 illustrates some of the questions raised by the theme in this book. These are by no means exhaustive.

The theme looks at countries as political and economic entities and offers a useful context for developing many geographical skills and concepts. It involves designing maps and diagrams; looking at relief, landscape features and climate; exploring how an area develops as a result of human and economic activity; land use and conflict of interest over land use; the exploitation of resources; use and misuse of natural resources; environmental issues etc. We suggest these issues be explored in the context of a tropical locality.

As well as touching on the English ATs, the simulation gives scope for drama and role play, for debating issues, asking questions and exploring ideas. Skills in media education will also be developed.

An emphasis is placed on how many present day countries were formed because of European activity in the last century. This work fulfils the history ATs and could fall within the study unit on the Victorians or in a school designed study unit.

The approach

This section explores why it is important to teach about the world outside Britain in the primary school. A checklist for planning is offered on the opposite page.

Why teach about other places?

Children from a very early age are aware of and interested in what is happening in the world outside their own locality. As stated in the Interim Report to the Geography Working Group[2]; '...*by the time they go to school, most of today's children are aware of distant places from the television screen*'. We would argue that:

- Young children have a very keen interest in distant places. This is particularly true in an age of mass communication, travel and migration when they are exposed to people and events from different places on a daily basis.

- Some children have personal experiences of life in distant places, through being part of a community with some of its roots in another part of the world, or through extended travel to visit family. For some, the distant may be more familiar than the local.

- Children do not learn about the world in a linear way. The process of trying to make sense of the world is organic and will naturally include reference to distant places.

- Making artificial divisions between the local and global may only serve to reinforce an understanding which is based on differences rather than similarities. Interdependence is a vital concept to build from the very early years of education.

- The distant can have a lot of appeal for children because it seems exotic and fantastic. If we can design a project which builds on this interest but challenges the idea of the exotic, children will be motivated to learn about another place.

Designing a theme about one country

There are many different ways of building on children's interest in and awareness of the wider world. One of the standard ways in which we teach about the wider world in the primary school is by taking another country as a focus for learning. If tackled well, this approach has tremendous potential for interesting as well as challenging children. Teaching about one country can be a concrete way of raising awareness about issues which face the wider world as a whole. It can also serve to focus children's attention on the news and newspapers.

Looking at how one country has developed solutions to its own needs over thousands of years will help create a positive image of a people active in their own development.

However, if it is not structured carefully, a project about another country can often serve to reinforce stereotyped ideas. This often arises out of a lack of clarity at the planning stages. If we are not clear what we want the children to gain from such a theme, it can end up being a bit of a mixed bag of activities about, for example, Indian clothes and food with a bit of history and geography thrown in.

A group of teachers planning to run a course on teaching about other places devised the chekclist opposite. You might use it in your staff group as starting point for your own discussions. What would you add to it or take from it?

There are some approaches to avoid when teaching about developing countries. This list, produced by CWDE [3] sums them up:

Teaching about 'developing' countries: a checklist of approaches to avoid.

1. *The tourist -eye view*
Is everything portrayed as quaint and curious? Is there an emphasis on elephants and snake-charmers and the exotic? Are the local community or members of the class used merely as audio-visual aids for a project on the country they originate from?

2. *The packet-of-tea approach*
Are people overseas shown as existing to grow our tea/cotton/sugar, or to provide us with exciting holidays? Is it implied that this is a very convenient arrangement: they are happy natives singing in the sunshine and we are happy tea-drinkers snug around the fire at home?

3. *The pathological view*
Is everything shown as absolutely desperate: people everywhere are dying of starvation, floods, hurricanes earthquakes? Are we shown as the only ones able to rescue them from such disaster?

4. *The pat on the head*
Is it implied that 'they' have been a bit behind with their mud huts and things but if they follow our example they'll come out right in the end? Is it implied that high technology, fast cars, automated industry, are the things that make a country 'developed'?

5. *Poverty as an act of God*
Is poverty treated as something that is simply there although, of course, we deplore it? Are some of the fundamental causes of poverty given or only descriptions of its symptoms?

A checklist for planning to teach about other places

- What exactly am I hoping the children will learn?

- How much do I have to know about the economic situation, basic geography, religion, languages, issues relating to minority groups etc., beyond that which I'll be actually using in the classroom?

- How can I take my own understanding of the country further?

- How would I justify this work to myself/to my colleagues on educational grounds?

- Can I anticipate the children's immediate reactions to images? Do I know the images they already hold? How am I going to respond?

- How far do the materials I have represent the views and images the people hold about themselves and their country?

- How am I going to teach about this place in a way that will enable the children to identify with the people's experiences?

- Am I primarily teaching about the people or the place?

- What are my images of the place/people? Are they fixed images? Where do they come from?

- If I have visited this country, what are the limitations of my experience?

- How comfortable would I feel if a teacher from this country were a 'fly on the wall' in my classroom?

- How far should I follow the interests of the children rather than stick to my original plan? In following their interests, is there a danger of reinforcing their stereotypes?

- What oversimplifications have I made? Can I justify these?

- Does what I have planned address important ordinary life experiences and social issues, as opposed to only addressing 'exotic culture'?

Finding out about a real country

This theme looks at the nature of a country and at the relationships between countries. It can also offer a real context for finding out about one country in greater depth.

In the early stages of planning a theme about another country, you will probably gather together appropriate resources. If it is a place you do not know, it can be tempting to rely heavily on the printed word for information. Much has been documented about the bias to be found in children's books. *Censoring reality* [4] is based on the search by a twelve year old child for information about South Africa. The report uncovers the overt and covert bias in most of the materials she comes across and the almost complete omission of the issue of apartheid. This may seem an extreme example, but it alerts us to the need to recognise the bias of the resources we are using.

We need to be aware of these biases ourselves and enable children to recognise them. *Hidden Messages?* [5] offers some practical classroom activities for exploring bias in books. Strategies are also offered for staff groups to formulate their own policy on book selection.

There are many other sources which offer background information on 'your country'. Try your local Development Education Centre, or development agencies such as Oxfam, Trocaire, CAFOD, Save the Children Fund and Christian Aid. The New Internationalist magazine contains interesting articles on issues and places. Addresses can be found on page 111.

While many of the glossy information books about different countries are an invaluable resource; others can be over generalised. Encyclopaedias, in particular, become outdated very quickly. The World Council of Churches [6] has issued guidelines suggesting what to look for in a book about one of the countries of the South [or 'Third World' countries]:

*   *Strong role models of 'Third world' people making their own decisions;*
*   *Customs and traditions presented in a way which explains their meaning from the point of view of the people involved;*
*   *Family relationships portrayed in a warm supportive way;*
*   *An emphasis on people rather than physical geography-people who speak for themselves;*
*   *Efforts of people to secure their own liberation are seen as valid;*
*   *Good quality illustrations or photographs;*
*   *Inclusion of controversial issues;*
*   *An emphasis on ordinary life rather than the exotic or unusual.*

The books shown here are examples of ones which give information about a people or place.

are passports and visas needed?

is the country finding its own solutions to its problems?

was it as you expected it to be?

Can you locate them on a map?

is this biased in any way?

have you lived in or visited another country?

by whom?

where can you find information?

what experience do you have of other countries?

how were they created?

Can you find out about a real country?

how important are the boundaries and borders of a country?

Can you create a country?

What is a country

how is your country inter-dependent?

what is it like to live there?

is it part of a continent?

Can you represent your country?

what physical features does it have?

what's the climate?

what special concerns does it face if it's an island?

on a map?

in other ways?

does it have raw materials?

does it sell cash crops?

how does it trade?

can you design and make an artefact to represent your country?

are there a diversity of lifestyles in your country?

what does it trade?

do separate communities live together peacefully?

is it fair trade?

does the symbolism raise any issues?

if not, what are the difficulties?

if not, why not?

how does it get on with its neighbours?

how do they resolve their conflicts?

53

The theme : What is a country?

This theme is designed around an extended activity in which children create their own countries and explore the concepts of interdependence and identity. Many issues about people and places arise naturally out of the simulation; some, such as colonialism and trade, are explored here.

Brainstorms*

You might introduce this work by using a couple of brainstorms* with the whole class. This will give you a good indication of the concepts the children are already starting from. You may find yourself surprised by what the children already know.

Brainstorm first 'What I need to live'. These are examples of the things some first and second year juniors come up with: money, food, water, jobs, houses, shelter, laws, power, electricity, education, hospitals, shops, transport, protection, police and mum. Concepts of production and religion were noticeable by their absence. Another class grasped the importance of friends, family and community easily, one child said 'I would be lonely without anyone to talk to'.

What is a country?

Next, brainstorm 'What is a country?'. You might find that the children get confused between a country and the countryside. Using a globe may help overcome this. These brainstorms can provide an evaluative tool; repeat them at the end of the project and see what the children have learnt. Opposite are some of the ideas that second and third year juniors came up with.

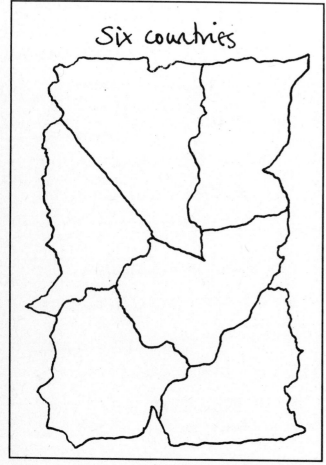

As a way of introducing this work, the children who had visited another country were interviewed by the rest of the class to find out about their experiences. Many of the children had been to Pakistan, India, Bangladesh and Jamaica. The aim was to illustrate how much we can learn by listening to other's experiences and that other places are different but not always in the ways we expect.

The activity gave status to the children's experiences in another country and at times surprised the rest of the class: 'I didn't think it was like that.' It was interesting to hear how often the children said it was just like being here.

This was followed up by looking at books about the country in question and this highlighted the issue of perception and bias. It might also have been good for the children to bring in items which they had brought back from their visit.

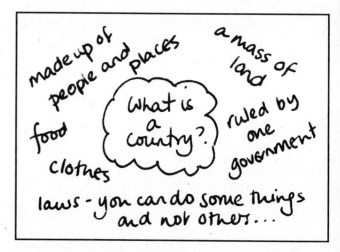

Creating an imaginary country

One way of taking the children's thinking further is to get them to create their own country and imagine what it is like to live there. Draw six shapes on a large piece of sugar paper or card. Each is to represent a country. They should connect together as countries do on a map. Cut out each of the shapes.

Divide children into mixed ability groups of about four with one shape per group. Tell them that each shape represents a country: their country. **Don't** show the whole or indicate that they fit together.

Some practical suggestions:
- Make each country really large (at least A3 size).
- Make original shapes as card templates, then make sugar paper copies. Any disasters can be remedied by replacement pieces - and you have an original which fits together - and you know how it goes.
- Mark which way up each shape is intended to be used.

What do we want to know about our country?

In groups brainstorm* what you want to know about your country - you may need to start with a whole class brainstorm. Bring all the groups to share their questions, thus pooling their resources. This list was produced by a group of juniors at Lauriston primary school in Hackney:

What do we eat?
What kinds of animals are there?
how many people live there?
are there many children?
What plants grow there?
is it flat?
is their food healty?
are they clean?
are they tidy?
are their colours the same?
What kind of clothes do they wear?
is it a dry or wet or hot country?
is it all countryside or all city?
is there a hospital?
are there shops?
is there sea around our country?
do they were shoes?
Where do they sleep?
are they rich?
are they poor?
where do they get their food from?
what are things made out of?
do they have sweets?
are they working always?
do they have toys?
are they busy?
do they talk the same language?
are their people living their?
what kind of transport is there?

Imagining answers

Having created an imaginary country, the groups need to build up some more information about it. These are some ways of putting the flesh on the skeleton.

Groups can do this by writing about aspects of their country, or representing some of their country's characteristics on their shape. Role play* is a valuable technique for imagining what it is like to live there. This is an ideal opportunity to offer a meaningful context for basic geographical work about climate, mapping, resources, land use, economic activity etc. The groups should answer obvious questions such as:

What is the name of your country?
What climate does it have?
What physical features e.g. rivers, mountains?
What raw materials?
What do they eat?

Practical considerations

- Issues of representation and symbol arise here. Leave groups to develop their own ideas as far as possible, but support their work by clarifying issues and problems the group present for solution.
- The class can benefit from general guidance such as putting in physical features first.
- Paint makes 'maps' more attractive. If groups feel very adventurous, they could construct their map in 3-D, using clay or junk modelling
- This is a major stage of the work - allow enough time for the children to develop their ideas.

You might also ask groups to think about what has happened in the past in their country which might link to the present situation. Links could be made with the ideas on colonialism on pages 60-63. Relate some of the learning points to real examples of countries.

Diversity

Most countries, if not all, are made up of people from different groups. These may be, for example, tribal groups such as the Mandinka in The Gambia and Senegal, or they may be groups who have originated from another part of the world and from minority groups in the country. This could be introduced by asking children to identify the groups who live in their country, the languages they speak, their traditions etc. Ideas in the *Roots and journeys* section might be useful here.

Nationalism?

By this stage, it is likely that the children's identification with their country will grow. One class of children became very nationalistic, with groups arguing 'our country is best'. It might be wise to prepare the children beforehand for this element of competition. This not only serves the purpose of the activity, but it also can be useful material for considering and discussing 'them' and 'us', 'insider' and 'outsider' issues in the classroom and in the world.

Here are two countries, which groups of children constructed, described in their own words.

Shancarseanaine

We are particularly happy with the pollution in our atmosphere because 98% of it is clean.

The people of our country are called Shancarseanaines.

The weather in Shancarseanaine is a mixture between sun and rain. We like it like that because our crops grow nice and fresh.

The hospitals are quite poor in Shancarseanaine are quite poor because we,ve only 2 doctors and 4 ambalances.

It is quite easy to get a job but The money is quite poor.

There are lots of schools and they all give you a good education.

The people of Shancarseanaine drive on the left-hand side of the road.

The most serious problem in our country is to do with finance because the government does not have enough money to back us up.

by; Carlo, Lorraine, Sean, Ann-Marie & Sharon.

Ceberia

Ceberia is not as big as England. We have rare wild animals and three polluted lakes.

Our money is called Jems and Frasers. 4 Jems make a Fraser.

Our wild animals are Dodo-birds, cheetahs and koala bears.

We have got one rainforest but most of our trees are being cut down.

The capital of Ceberia is Cebrin.

We have got four main hospitals and ten little hospitals but three of them are still under construction.

The government is paying for the hospitals.

Our most serious problem is that the rainforest is being cut down.

Our first most important rule is that you drive on the right-hand side of the road.

Our second most important rule is that you leave school at the age of 18.

Our third most important rule is that you have to go away to get an education.

by: Brian, Vicky, John-Paul and Siobhan

Anthems and artefacts

These activities can be used to deepen and share understanding about life in a different country.

Countries generally have a national anthem, a flag, currency, stamps etc. If time permits there are all kinds of avenues to pursue here. If your country were to start a tourist trade, what would it sell? How would you attract visitors? What kinds of postcards would you have? These are two examples of postcards which children drew. The Images section offers possibilities for extending this work.

Objects
One way of beginning to find out about a community is to look at the artefacts, or objects which they use. It is important to recognise the limitations as well as the value of using artefacts. The very term 'artefact' can imply something different, possibly exotic. Using the term 'objects' with children may encourage them to think the ordinary rather than the unusual.

A group of teachers who travelled to Ghana collected a range of objects to bring home and use in school. One item which raised much discussion was the plastic bucket, identical to the ones you buy in any hardware shop here. It highlighted the similarity rather than difference between lifestyles.

You might introduce this work by asking the children to decide which ten objects they would use to tell someone from another place about their classroom. Imagine that the items are to be sent by air and therefore have to be packed in a small shoe box. It fairly quickly becomes clear that there are huge limitations on what you can send! Ask them to think about the messages which the receivers might pick up from their selection. Is there a chance of misinterpretation?

They could collect a small set of artefacts which might be used in 'their country' to explain a little about life there. Can they construct their own artefacts using simple technology?

Checklists
A useful reinforcement of the learning so far, and preparation for the next set of activities is to give each group a checklist of questions about their country. These should include basic physical and social dimensions: e.g. climate, resources, education, health, rules and transport. The group will need to be able to talk about these things to a visitor.

A visit
Ask each group to select one member to visit another 'country', find out about it and report back. Discuss how to welcome visitors, how it feels to go somewhere new. Groups exchange visitors, who must ask, listen and remember what they find out without writing it down and then return to their own country with information.

For one class involved in extensive work on this theme, the visit was a high point in the project. This piece of role-play was fully entered into by the children, who really wanted to communicate and find out about each other's countries.

Another class spend quite a lot of time debriefing the experience of 'visiting' a country as one of the visiting children had not been made welcome. This led to quite a lot of discussion about the hostility we can feel when we go to strange places. *Rafa Rafa†* is a useful simulation game for exploring cross cultural communication and misunderstanding.

In the hot seat
Each group in turn, with only their map for support, sits at the front of the class. First, they introduce their country with the aid of their 'map'. Then, the rest of the class 'interview' them about various features of life there. Each questioner must present a different question.

Invariably, additional aspects of life arise which the group have not discussed. The group may improvise. These new elements provide a fresh level of discussion e.g. 'What religion do you have?'.

At this stage the whole class can brainstorm* a list of what are the essential things which make up a country. This will probably include people, government, a law keeping force, shelter, a means of food production, raw materials etc. Review the brainstorm and see if there is anything which is not essential to make up a country.

A jigsaw

Individual countries are connected to each other, as continents or through other relationships such as trade. This has implications for how adjacent countries relate to each other. These activities begin to explore the notion of interdependence of countries.

Pin the country shapes randomly on the board and ask the children if they can see any connections between them. They will probably see that the shapes fit together. Ask several children to fit them together to form one continent or land mass. What changes does this make to the ideas they had about their country? The class will probably need to agree to change features which do not make sense now the countries are joined e.g. rivers may need to join up or start in different places; mountain ranges don't usually stop at a border; railway and transport communications may need to be altered.

Countries are not only linked together physically, they are also linked in other ways. Brainstorm* in groups as many ways as you can in which countries are connected to each other. Feed these back to the whole class.

Pollution was a key issue for one class, once their countries had been joined. One country had developed industrially, creating pollution in rivers which flowed into another. Smoke from their factories was also an issue for concern for its neighbours. This illustrates how this theme can be a powerful tool for tapping into the children's own concerns.

Advantages or disadvantages?
What are the advantages and disadvantages of the countries being linked? Groups could list these from their previous brainstorm. Alternatively, you could photocopy the comments shown here and the children sort* them into two sets.

Feedback to the whole class and discuss the major points that come up. This may also be an appropriate time to talk about some of the things which make one country poor and another rich. You will also need to make sure that children understand that within any one country there is diversity; this may be from city life to rural life, a range of 'ethnic' groups, poverty and wealth etc. These are very big questions and you will need to allow plenty of time for discussion.

Changing it all!
Ask the children to imagine that the six countries are bound together in one continent, surrounded by sea. You want to make sure that all the people in the whole continent are able to live peacefully and well. What changes need to be made? This could be undertaken in the original groups of four or as a class.

An island
Some countries are not joined to a main land mass and form islands. Another way of organising your six countries is to have five joined and one an island. What differences would this make to that country. What would be the advantages and disadvantages of living on an island? You can illustrate that by looking at a particular island such as Barbados, Zanzibar etc.

receiving food or money if you have problems

being able to buy food or raw materials if you run out, or if there is a famine

polluting the environment of another country

being able to buy food which doesn't grow in your country

being able to sell extra food you don't need

taking over (colonising) another country

being taken over (colonised) by another country

going to war with another country

escaping to live in another country

moving to another country to get new jobs

meeting people who have different traditions

learning new languages and stories

travelling to a different climate for a holiday

Trading

Countries make links with each other by trading. One country has something which another needs, so they swap items. As time goes on a more sophisticated system is likely to develop.

The trading game†
There are many ways of fostering children's understanding of trading. A simulation game published by Christian Aid called *The trading game*† can be an excellent introduction. The game involves dividing the class into groups which represent countries of varying economic power. Each country is given certain items at the beginning of the game. The two rich countries are given scissors, a pair of compasses, pens, ruler, protractors [to represent technology] and a small amount of paper [to represent raw materials]. The middle income countries are given less 'technology' and more raw materials. The low income countries have the most raw materials but hardly any 'technology'.

The aim of the game is to make money by manufacturing shapes which can be banked for different amounts. The shapes are constructed, by geometry or by drawing around set squares etc. Trading automatically takes place as countries cannot make many shapes without acquiring more raw materials or technology. You might make your own game up using similar principles. If constructing shapes using geometric skills is too difficult, the children could use logi blocks as templates.

Bananas!
One of the issues which *The trading game*† illustrates well is that trading is not necessarily a fair process. Some groups may start at an advantage to others. This is borne out in the real world where many of the producers of crops end up with a tiny proportion of the final profit. This is well illustrated by 'The banana game' in the handbook *World studies 8-13* [7]. Many teachers have used this as a simulation game in the classroom. Others have used it to illustrate the point in school assemblies. *Go bananas*† contains photographs and activities to look at issues of interdependence and trading in relation to the banana industry.

Sowing and harvesting†
Some communities have to decide whether they are going to grow food for their own needs or whether they need to grow extra food to sell in order to obtain money they need for items they cannot grow. *Sowing and harvesting*† is an excellent game which children can play to look at these issues to build on the concept of trading.

Trading in Mali

A top junior class had been doing some work on Mali. The project began with an 'archaeological dig' in which the children 'found' some artefacts which told what people's lives were like in ancient Mali. These included kola nuts, beads, tools for cutting salt etc. The class also did quite a lot of map work on Mali and saw the different regional ways of living.

As a result of this work, the children built up the concept of what was valuable in that particular society. In small groups, they were given slips of paper indicating which group of people they were and where they lived e.g. the forest people, the savanna people etc. Their paper also told them what resources they had and what they would need to survive. These included camels, kola nuts, salt, gold, glass beads, fabrics, spices etc. Different groups needed different items.

Some resources were readily available to all groups, e.g. kola nuts, but others like camels were less available. The children automatically traded. Some found that they had things that others wanted. When the game was over, in the debriefing they realised that trading involved:

- *travelling;*
- *having a recognised meeting place;*
- *shouting about what you have;*
- *protecting what you have! Some people had to stay at home;*
- *developing certain recognised ways of trading e.g. a certain number of kola nuts could be exchanged for a camel.*

Why do people trade?

to get things they need or would like to have

to sell extra things they have too many of

for extra cash – to make money

as a way of travelling

to make a living

to meet people e.g. at market

Borders

Many peoples have had the experience of having arbitrary borders imposed on them by others. These activities explore this idea.

Introduce this by asking the children to think about why one country might want to take over another. If feelings of nationalism and self protection came out earlier in creating a country these could act as a useful point of reference. If you want to tie this work in directly with the children's own countries, you could announce that one of the countries has taken over two of the others. Each country could brainstorm* what it feels like in their position:

- *to be taken over;*
- *to take over another country;*
- *to watch your neighbours being taken over.*

Debrief this carefully, perhaps referring to real situations where this has happened.

Borders

One the striking things when we look at a tribal map of Africa, is to see that the borders go right through tribal lands. The Maasai's land was divided by the Kenya/Tanzania border. In West Africa the Mandinka's land spans The Gambia and Senegal; there is a local saying that every Senegalese has a Gambian cousin. These borders were constructed by the European powers at the Congress of Berlin in 1884-5, reflecting the already established interests of the European powers. They did not fit in with the history and politics of the African peoples.

The 'countries' activity will have shown how borders cut through natural features such as rivers and plains; you might simulate this by adding borders across the shapes without negotiating with the children. How did they feel when this happened? This can be used to illustrate the arbitrary nature of the dividing up of Africa.

The map opposite shows the political borders of Africa. Behind the creation of many of these borders lie interesting stories which raise issues about the arbitrary nature of country boundaries. You might use the map with children to illustrate some of those stories. Are there other examples which you can find?

The Gambia/Senegal
The British had trading links on either side of the river Gambia. They did not want to give up this area as most of West Africa had been colonised by the French and the British wanted to keep some power there. The borders of The Gambia were drawn to follow the path of the river and not the interests of the local people.

Tanzania/Kenya
Originally Mount Kilimanjaro, the highest mountain in Africa, was in Kenya. Kenya had been colonised by England. Queen Victoria, the queen of England, wanted to give her German cousin a gift. Germany had colonised Tanzania, so she gave him Mt. Kilimanjaro. The border changed so that the mountain is now in Tanzania.

Libya/Egypt : Namibia/Botswana
These are two example of borders which are straight lines; they do not follow any geographical feature, such as a river or mountain range. They follow the lines of latitude.

Namibia/Zambia
The shape of Namibia is very unusual, with a long thin strip of land in the north east. The Germans who colonised Namibia wanted to be able to get to the Zambezi river which flowed through Zambia. They wanted to use the river for trade. The border was made to fit their wish.

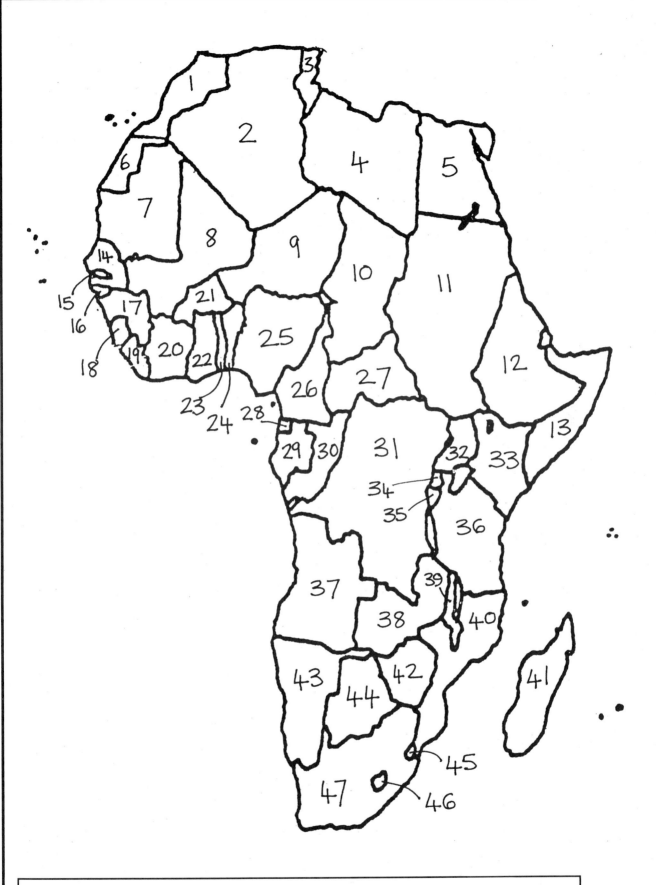

1 Morrocco	11 Sudan	21 Burkino Faso	31 Zaire	41 Madagascar
2 Algeria	12 Ethiopia	22 Ghana	32 Uganda	42 Zimbabwe
3 Tunisia	13 Somalia	23 Togoland	33 Kenya	43 Namibia
4 Libya	14 Senegal	24 Benin	34 Rwanda	44 Botswana
5 Egypt	15 Gambia	25 Nigeria	35 Burundi	45 Swaziland
6 Western Sahara	16 Guinea-Bissau	26 Cameroun	36 Tanzania	46 Lesotho
7 Mauritania	17 Guinea	27 Central African Republic	37 Angola	47 South Africa
8 Mali	18 Sierra Leone	28 Equatorial Guinea	38 Zambia	
9 Niger	19 Liberia	29 Gabon	39 Malawi	
10 Chad	20 Ivory Coast	30 Congo	40 Mozambique	

These photographs are taken from a colour photopack concerned with teaching about Kenya and Tanzania in the primary school [see resources list on page 64]. The accompanying teachers' handbook, suggests how to teach about issues such as self reliance, tourism, colonialism and land use through practical classroom activities.

Being colonised

A country which is colonised by another, is usually forced to change its way of life to fit in with that of the colonising country.

This activity explores what it might mean to be colonised by the French. We have chosen France because it is a country which was involved in the colonial process in the last century, and because it is a place about which children are likely to have some knowledge. It is a foreign power and therefore it can also help us to reflect on how we might feel if we were colonised. These statements show some of the consequences if you are colonised by the French. They could be adapted for any colonising power, including those countries which the children have created.

Give each group the statements on slips of paper. Explain to them that their country has to be colonised by the French and these are some of the results. Ask each groups to sort* their statements into two piles: advantages and disadvantages. They can then pick out the greatest advantage and the greatest disadvantage of being colonised.

Discuss with the class what it might be like to be colonised. You can use the class discussion as a basis for a role play* of the colonisation of a fictional country, for example one of your six.

The French are in power, they make the laws which are based on those in France.

The French get the top jobs.

Your customs and culture are seen as inferior to the French.

They build roads, ports and railways so that the colony can trade with the 'mother country'.

You have to speak French to get jobs.

If you go to school, you learn French.

Your land is taken away from you, partly or completely.

You have to grow food which is exported from France.

You have to follow the religion of France.

You are introduced to money for the first time.

The French establish a health and education system.

You become part of an Empire and a trading system.

Resources: What is a country?

An Arctic child, an active learning pack for 8-13 year olds, Greenlight Publications, 1988.
This pack examines our relationship with the Arctic and some of its peoples - the Inuit and the Sami. It aims to see something of the area's beauty through their eyes and to understand the threats to sustainable development.

Beans series A&C Black, various dates and titles.
This series explores the lives of ordinary people, both past and present in different parts of the world. Each book is designed for children and focuses on the life of one child.

Caribbean fishermen, Rex Walford, Cambridge Publishing Services, 1986.
A simulation game set on an imaginary island in the Caribbean which looks at the precarious choices fishermen have to make. Players have to choose whether to fish on shore or off shore; the key factor, the weather, is decided by the throw of a dice.

Disasters in the classroom, teaching about disasters in the third world, Leeds DEC, 1989.
How can teachers approach work on 'natural disasters' without reinforcing negative images about the countries of the South? This pack offers ideas for examining the causes which underlie any disaster. A useful way of following up images work.

East Africa photopack, DEC, 1991.
This forthcoming pack, designed for upper juniors, looks at issues of development through colour photographs and theme work. The pack focuses on tourism, land use, trade and self reliance. It has been developed by a group of primary teachers who travelled to Kenya and Tanzania on a study visit.

Geography in the primary school, John Bale, Routledge and Kegan Paul, 1987.
Practical ideas for teachers about introducing geographical skills into the primary classroom. This book reviews children's 'private geographies' and suggests how teachers can build on these using particular learning strategies.

Go bananas! a photoset and activities about the journey of a banana for primary and middle schools, Oxfam, 1990.
Focusing on how bananas are grown in St Vincent and transported for sale in the U.K., this pack offers a wide range of practical activities for discussing issues which arise from the inequality of trading.

Rafa rafa, Garry Shirts, Simile 11 California, available from Christian Aid, 1976.
A simulation game which deals with issues of newness, difference and cross cultural communication. It simulates real life situations such as moving to a new situation. Players are divided into two groups, Alphas and Betas who separately learn their rules and customs. The two groups exchange visitors, who try to join the activity of the host culture, which is not as easy as it sounds!

Sowing and harvesting, Oxfam, 1989.
This game, for juniors is designed to introduce the relationship between cash and food crops and to show how cash cropping can lead to a lack of food for the producers.

Teaching development issues - Perceptions, Colonialism, Food, Health, Population Changes, Work, Aid and Development, Manchester DEP, 1986.
A series of handbooks for secondary teachers about global issues. The activities, stimulus sheets and statistics can be adapted for use with younger children, for example, a page in *Colonialism* shows Trafalgar Square the links it has with the Moslem Arabs.

The trading game, Christian Aid, 1986.
This lively game for up to 30 players can be used to help players to understand how trading takes place and how people begin at different starting points. Maths skills are used to create shapes for trading.

Clean water, a right for all, active project work for 8-13 year olds, Unicef - UK, 1989.
This teacher's handbook illustrates how an issue such as the lack of access to safe water which is commonly thought of as applying to mainly poor countries, has relevance to everyday lives in this country. The materials contain photocopiable sheets and photographs.

We are what we eat! - but who controls our choice? UNICEF, 1989.
A practical handbook addressing issues of a healthy diet and food supply around the world. It starts from the assumption that adverse environmental conditions often trigger or exacerbate a food shortage but are not usually the sole cause of people starving.

Where does our food come from?, Oxfam, Christian Aid, Scholastic publications, 1989.
A full colour poster showing where many of the everyday items which fill our shopping baskets come from. Teacher's notes supply background information.

The world feast game, Christian Aid, 1988.
By trading, making a mural and eating the food they have produced, children are encouraged to question the way the world's food is shared out. Suitable for a class of juniors.

World in a supermarket bag, Oxfam, 1987.
An activity sheet which can be used to explore where our food comes from, the real cost of food and how food travels. It is designed to generate discussion about the different relative costs of food and what trade means.

Roots and journeys

Immigrant
[for Rebecca and Rhina]
From mangrove and swamp her
    forefathers
hacked this rugged land;
    laid tracks
townships, roads and ports.
    With wife
and child in tow, sweated
    blood
in tin mine and rubber estate
    to give
this country its spine of steel.

In the teeth of disease, death
    torture
her fathers fought from the
    heart
of our deepest, darkest jungle
    to wrest
this land from the martial
    fist
of the occupying imperialist.

Her mothers' wit, inventiveness
    genius
enriched our language, culture
    cuisine
with cake, curry, kebaya, boria
    porcelain.

Her roots now so entwined with
    strands
of this country's history/future
    she felt
not one iota less than a full
    citizen.
Till that fateful morning when
    she awoke
to find herself branded **immigrant.**

Cecil Rajendra, *taken from Dove on fire [1]*

Societies are dynamic, changing and are influenced as new groups of people settle. They bring their food, clothes and technology; their language, values and religion. As people from different traditions settle together in the same place, issues such as conflict of interest, power relationships and racism often arise. This theme offers a framework for children to explore their own personal histories and roots. These can then be set in the wider context of movement and settling. Particular emphasis is put on the diverse nature of our own society.

In the national curriculum
We have chosen to focus the activities in this section on history, geography, English, science and personal/social education/RE. The web on page 69 illustrates some of the questions raised by the theme in this book. These are by no means exhaustive.

Roots and journeys offers an excellent context for studying how and why people have travelled over the years. It addresses concepts such as immigration, emigration, invasion, settlement, conquest, exploration, trade and navigation. It could be used to explore ideas in History Study Units 2, 4, 5, 7, 8, 10, 11 and 12 and each history AT.

Parallel to the historical work in this theme, we have developed a focus on geographical skills and concepts. These include map work, scale and distance, the relationship between places, why people journey and the effects of population movement and settlement.

As well as offering an important context for developing children's skills in English ATs 1, 2 and 3, *Roots and journeys* offers scope for looking at other issues which relate particularly to language. The way language travels and changes over time and distance; different written scripts; diaries are suggested as a form of recording; drama, role play and stories are suggested as media for looking at issues relating to journeys.

Myths and stories through which communities express their beliefs about how life began, offer a valuable lead into RE, as does work on religious journeys such as the pilgrimage and haji. Other work on roots looks at personal identity, family histories and scientific investigations around AT2, the variety of life.

The approach

This section explores some of the issues to think about when planning a theme on roots and journeys. It looks at how maps can be used to enable children to develop a global dimension and at the importance of including a range of perspectives in a theme such as exploration.

Map work skills

An important element of developing a global perspective is that children acquire some skills in reading maps.

These are some of the map work skills which children can usefully develop:

- to be able to 'read' a map, understanding what different lines, shadings and symbols mean;
- to understand that there is a variety of landscape and lifestyle in any area;
- to understand how scale and distance on a map relate to the real world;
- an understanding of the relationship between distance and the time needed to travel;
- to understand that the borders on maps are created by people;
- to see where places are located in relation to each other;
- to begin to build up their own 'mental map' of the world.

Scale and distance

In order to begin to read maps children need some understanding of the idea of scale and distance. This is probably best introduced by using local maps, say of the classroom, the school or the local area. The class could make their own maps of the classroom or the playground. Can they draw a map to scale?

Find a 'local kilometre' with which the children are all familiar, e.g. from the school to the library, or from the bus stop to the post office. Use this as a reference point for larger distances, [so London is 200 'library walks' from Birmingham]. With this 'tool', look at some of the distances on a map.

Cities, countries and continents.

To overcome confusion about whether a place name refers to a city, a country or a continent give groups slips of paper on each of which is written a place name, e.g. London, Asia, India, Nigeria, Moscow. Can they sort* them into cities, countries and continents? Check their choices with an atlas.

Children often think that Africa is a country rather than a continent. Ask them to sort slips of paper with names of countries on into those they think are in Africa and those which are not. Use the map on page 61 to check their choices out. You might try this with other countries and continents.

Getting used to maps

There are lots of simple games to help children familiarise themselves with the idea of maps and with where places are located. It is always worth having a map or globe in the classroom on view.

- Each day choose 3 places on the map/globe for the children to locate, in any spare moment. Talk about the places with the whole class at the same time each day. Children could choose for each other.

- Put up questions relating to the map, e.g.
  Which countries are on the borders of Chile?
  Which is larger, Kenya or The Gambia?
  Which country is the odd one out...Argentina, Colombia, Korea, Paraguay and Brazil?

- Trace one of the countries on the world map and cut out a template. Can the children guess which country it is? Can they make their own template for their friends to guess?

- **Which country am I?** Give the children five clues about a place and see if they can find out where it is e.g.:
  I am a country north of the equator
  I am to the east of the USA
  I have no borders on the sea
  One of my borders is on Lake Chad
  My capital is Niamey

Once children are used to referring to the large map or globe, they can devise their own games for each other. They will also probably want to look at atlases and see places in greater detail.

Match the photos!

It can be difficult to imagine what the area represented by a map looks like on the ground. Use a photoset, such as the set on Kenya and Tanzania, [see page 62] or *Water* [2] to bring the map to life. Ask the children to imagine where on the map they think each photograph could have been taken. Use clues, such as whether the land is arid, whether the photo shows a city or village. Some will be easier to place than others. What is important is that children are able to interpret information from the map, not whether their answers are exactly right.

Many of the ideas in *What is a country?* lend themselves to developing mapping skills.

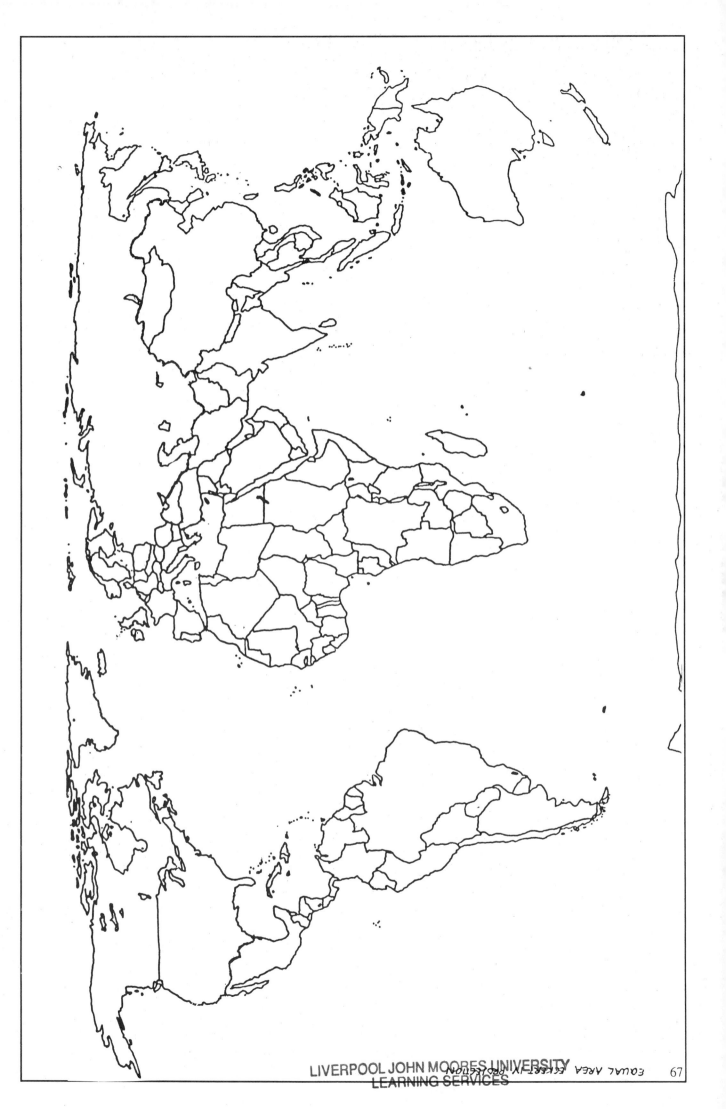

Exploration and encounter - a range of perspectives

Roots and journeys offers a cross curricular context in which to look at the common primary theme, 'exploration'.

Drawing on historical and geographical dimensions, *Roots and journeys* is a valuable starter for taking children outside their own experiences. It can be used to develop children's understanding of exploration, settlement, immigration, emigration, trade and conquest as set out in several of the national curriculum history themes. These concepts can be illustrated with examples from different periods in history, such as the experiences of invaders and settlers [Romans, Anglo-Saxons and Vikings]; immigration and emigration in Victorian Britain; exploration and encounter with the wider world in the C15 and C16. They each teach us that Britain is a dynamic, multicultural society which has been influenced by many groups over thousands of years. *'The study of history is concerned with the causes and effects of these movements and their profound consequences for the shaping of British culture'.* [3]

Different interpretations

The history curriculum places a great deal of emphasis on the understanding of points of view and different interpretations of history [attainment target 2]. In 3.28[4] this is expanded upon:

'..understanding that some histories have a high profile, others are hardly known, yet others [like the differing roles of men and women] now are finding a place in the main arena of history.'

The implications of this are that it is vital that we include a range of historical points of view. The standard way in which children have learnt about exploration has promoted the perspectives of famous, powerful and usually white European men such as Marco Polo and Colombus. This has often resulted in certain groups of children feeling excluded, marginalised, or bored e.g. :

* *girls, because all the main characters they learn about are male;*
* *black children, because the only black people likely to appear are the native peoples who are 'discovered'.*

We need to address the racism and sexism underpinning this approach by drawing on a broader range of perspectives because:

* it will help children to grasp the concept of exploration in a fuller sense;
* it directly challenges a Eurocentric view of the world built on the notion of white supremacy;
* it promotes the experiences of groups who are either ignored or depicted in a patronising way;
* it encourages the self esteem of black children, girls and children from groups which are rarely given status;
* by tapping into alternative viewpoints you will be relating the work more closely to a wider range of children's experience;
* it is necessary in order to deliver the national curriculum.

A range of perspectives

In this theme you can ensure a range of perspectives by looking at the experiences and perspectives of three groups:

> the explorers,
> those who stayed behind,
> the host community.

The people who came† [about settlers and invaders in the Caribbean], *We are Mesquakie, we are one,†* and *Profile on prejudice†* [about the experiences of Native Americans] are worth referring to as sources.

Things to think about when planning a theme:

Women's perspectives

* Give examples of women who were active and dynamic in their own societies.
* Give value to women's lives in the home, the market, the fields, politics, as healers, spiritual leaders etc.
* Explore how women addressed sexism in their societies.

Ordinary lives

* Give examples of ordinary working people's lives. Use examples of their own stories.
* Look at experiences of work, home life, look at corporate struggles and achievements of working class people, e.g. through trade unions.
* Show how government policy changes affected people.

Black and minority perspectives

* Show how black people have been active in determining their own history.
* Offer black perspectives on events which are usually portrayed from white perspectives.
* Ensure that black people are shown as active participants.
* Look at the black communities in Britain over the centuries and in other parts of the world.

From the wider world

* Give examples of how people interacted between nations outside Europe, through trade, war, etc.
* Give value to the civilisations who developed long before the European ones.
* Avoid comparing societies and peoples to European ones.

---

why do people become exiles or refugees?

what's it like to live your life on the move as a traveller or nomad?

how did they navigate?

what's it like to be forcibly driven away from your home?

why? is it always a choice?

how?

why?

which communities explored new lands?

how did people travel in the past?

what journeys do we take?

what's the best mode of transport today?

why do people travel?

what was it like to be settled or invaded?

how do people journey?

what are your roots?

Roots and Journeys

— what's it like to move to a new place?

what does it feel like to be a stranger?

how important are they to you?

are you rooted in a community in another place?

which communities have journeyed to Britain?

why do people encounter prejudice?

what are the roots of the community you live in?

why did they come?

how do they deal with it?

who came? who stayed behind?

what did they leave behind?

how important are roots to us? plants?

how were they received?

why?

can you set up a fair test to show why?

what did they bring with them?

how does language travel?

what evidence is there for this in your local area?

The theme : Roots and journeys

This theme can be tackled from all kinds of angles. We suggest science investigations as one way in to looking at the theme. This can link into discussion of personal histories and then into issues of travelling, exploring, invading or settling.

Roots

There are many possible starting points for this theme. We suggest one place to begin is by scientific investigations around roots. As one of the standard spring and summer term themes, there are many materials around which give plenty of ideas to start on. These are a few possibilities.

Sorting*

In groups, children can observe different kinds or roots with magnifying glasses. These could include tap roots, buttress roots, fibrous roots, soft roots, aerial roots etc. Include foods which are roots, in particular foods which originate outside Britain. Sort* them into different sets. It is more challenging to sort into three sets as opposed to two!

Do plants need roots to survive?

Can the children devise a fair test to investigate the answer to this question? Can they grow roots in coloured dyes and see how this affects their growth? Build on the outcomes of these investigations by getting children to decide why roots are important. Brainstorm* the purpose of roots as a whole class. Tree roots are a good example for showing how roots keep a plant stable, from falling over. You could illustrate this with photographs of trees blown over by a high wind showing the roots torn from soil.

In a new spot

Transfer two plants which have roots into a new situation. This can be either outdoors or inside. Dig the soil carefully and place one plant in the soil with roots intact, cover it, water it and take care of it. The other plant should be left on the surface of the soil and not cared for. What do the children think might happen? Observe and record the effects over the next few weeks. Discuss what happened and why. Which was the most beneficial situation for the plant?

Parallels can be drawn between this and situations when people are uprooted and moved elsewhere. What does it feel like to go and live in a new place? Are there certain circumstances which makes it easier for people to settle in? Some of the stories on page can be used to explore this idea.

The 'roots' idea could be taken further by looking at their importance in the rainforest. *Science for survival* [5] has some excellent ideas which can be adapted for younger children. *Roots and shoots*† approaches the experience of school gardens in a global context.

Other profitable areas in this theme include looking at the roots of humanity in creation stories. *Worlds of difference*† tells stories from different religions and traditions.

IDENTITY CARD

Description

Nationality _____

Occupation _____

Place of birth _____   Date of birth _____

Country of residence _____

Height _____   Weight _____   Colour of eyes _____

Special peculiarities _____

Signature _____

Photograph or self portrait

My own 'roots'
Understanding the importance of roots for plants can form a useful starting point for children exploring their own 'roots'. It will depend on the amount of work you have undertaken previously in this area as to how much time you spend on personal 'roots' and journeys. If children are new to this kind of work, you might want to spend some time on looking at who they are, and what the influences are in their lives in an activity such as this.

Who am I?
Everyone is different, and we all have different experiences which make us 'me'. Ask the children to think about what these things are which have made them who they are. They could depict this by drawing a picture and labelling themselves, or drawing a wok/cooking pot and thinking about the ingredients that contribute to who they are. These 'roots' often come up when children do this activity:

gender	religion	friends
concerns	likes and dislikes	where I live
language	class	attitudes
where my family come from		

You might use this opportunity to talk about some of these categories further, for instance discuss whether the place where they live affects their identity.

All about me
Favourite objects can be useful indicators of our 'roots', or at least of something important about us. Ask the children to bring in one object from home which tells something about themselves. It could be a favourite toy, a picture or something quite ordinary which has great personal significance. Back in school they can explain to partner or to a small group about why their object is so important to them. This activity can bring out a new side to some children.

Some of the activities in the *Self Esteem* [6] books, along with activities from *Images* [page 84] and *Change* [pages 100 and 102] are also valuable starters. Family trees are a popular way of finding out your own 'roots'. Timelines* help map out personal 'roots' and possible futures. Talk about issues arising from them, such as:

- *What are the consequences of certain actions?*
- *What changes take place between generations?*
- *Are our 'roots' influenced by where we were born or where we live?*

Identity cards
Children could make their own identity cards or 'passports' to indicate some of their 'roots'. Fill in the description of yourself and the add a photograph or self portrait.

Where have we travelled?

Everyone in the class will have some experience of going on a journey even if it is only from home to school.

In groups, brainstorm* a list of journeys which the children have been on. Display a map and ask the children to identify places they have travelled to and why. You may need a local, national and/or world map depending on the experiences of the children. You might introduce the idea of a map with activities from page 66. A label with each child's name on could be linked to the area of the world or town by a piece of wool.

Build the map up by asking the children to find out and display where parents, grandparents, friends, other teachers have travelled. It is surprising how many links you can often find.

Where would you like to live?

Imagine you are flying in a balloon, high above the clouds. All the people you most want to live with are in the balloon. The balloon is going to land in the place you would like to live in most. Draw, write or talk to your friend about what that place is like. It can be a real place or one you have made up.

- What can you see?
- Are there people? What are they like?
- What are you going to do?
- What would you miss most about leaving the place you are living in now?

A balloon for grandad† could be used as a stimulus to this activity.

Why journey?

Groups of children can brainstorm* why people travel. Feed these back to the whole class and record the ideas on a large sheet of paper. Over the next few days, children can research [by looking at television or in newspapers, or by asking friends and relatives] and add other reasons to the class sheet. If all the examples of journeys are local ones, remind them that people travel across the world and have done for many years.

As a way of beginning to make sense of why people journey, ask the children to group them to see if there are any patterns e.g. 'religious journeys' such as the haji, or pilgrimages. There is plenty of scope for following the children's ideas and interests.

What to take ?

What would you would take with you on a particular journey? e.g. a school trip. or a camping holiday. You will need to stress that there is limited space and therefore they will have to think quite carefully about what to take, and what to leave. Discuss your choices and reasons for them.

Some people take very little with them on their journeys. Bedouin tribes people take a drinking vessel, tents and the Koran as their basics. Photocopy the bottom part of this page and give it to groups to discuss. What did Aboriginal peoples take with them? Can you find out more about Aboriginal and other travelling peoples from information books? Which peoples still travel in this way?

These drawings are pieces of traditional rock art by Aboriginals. Their rock art is a symbolic language showing human beings and their relationship with the environment.

Song maps

In the beginning, according to Australian Aborigine legends, the great Ancestors walked across the land and made everything in it. The Aborigines who followed lived in harmony with the land and the animals. They survived by eating wild plant foods, hunting small animals and fishing. They lived in small groups spaced across the land and regularly travelled to new places as the food supply dried up. They became skilled in knowing where food and water could be found, remembering this information by singing it into songs. These were called 'song maps' or 'song lines' because they described journeys across the landscape.

The Aborigines travelled on foot and had to carry all they needed on their journeys. They took very few possessions and the things they took often had many purposes:

wooden bowls - were used for carrying water, food or even babies;

woomera or spear thrower - a long board with a peg at one end into which the shaft or spear fitted. It could also be used as a chisel, a digging stick, a splint for broken bones and as a weapon.

Some Aborigines still live this traditional way of life, although many are finding it difficult to do so.

What we bring

When people go to live in another part of the world they take with them all kinds of things, not only concrete items but also language, values, religion, food, traditions, clothes etc. These influence the society into which they move.

A walk round the area

If you live in an area where there are visible signs of the things which people bring, e.g. a mosque, Chinese restaurants, signs in languages other than English etc. go for a walk round the area listing all the things which communities bring with them. Use the ideas for getting out and about* on page 47. Alternatively, use photographs of a multiracial area such as those in the *City images* [7] pack. Use these to talk about how ideas and objects travel. *Colonialism*† contains a stimulus sheet showing objects from Islamic culture as shown below.

Collecting connections

The class could make a collection of items which people have brought to this country in the recent and distant past. If this really takes off, you may find yourself with a classroom full of examples from pictures of Hadrian's wall and the local mosque, to packets of biscuits with Urdu and English text!

* *Can you trace which communities brought these items?*
* *Why did they come?*
* *When did they come?*
* *Where did they come from?*
* *Do you think they and their ideas were welcomed?*

Objects from Islamic Culture

COLONIALISM

This will help convey the concept that this is a changing society, influenced by all the communities who have come to live here over the centuries, and that many things which are taken for granted as part of 'the British way of life' have been brought by people from all over the world. *The Black makers of history series* [8] gives many examples of the achievements of people from all over the world through the ages, and can help challenge the notion that technological developments only took place in Europe.

The theme is also a useful starting point for challenging any notions that immigration is only a recent phenomena. *They came to Britain*† and *Black settlers*† offer useful background material. Another way of addressing this would be to trace which communities have come to live in Britain over a period of time and identify what they have brought with them. This idea can be developed in many ways to give value to the experiences and traditions which have been brought to enrich a society.

Welcome Poster

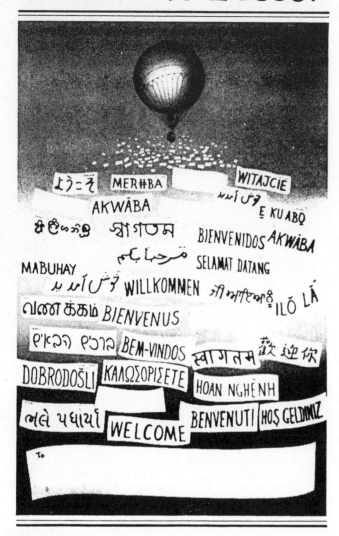

The ILEA Welcome poster is available from: Harcourt, Brace, Jovanovitch Ltd. Please see addresses on page 111.

Language

One contribution which incoming communities bring is that of language although in British society this can be seen as more of a problem than an asset. There is plenty of scope in this theme for language awareness work. It offers opportunities to value the knowledge and experience which bilingual children bring and to challenge negative ideas.

Finding scripts

Make a collection of labels, packets and leaflets in a range of languages and scripts. When a lower junior class made their own collection, they were amazed [as was their teacher] at the number of things that are labelled in more than one language. Local libraries often stock free leaflets in several scripts.

Cut up different scripts and sort them out so that each group will have a pile which includes several examples of the same script but from different sources. Can groups sort them into sets of text from the same language? How did they decide which went together? What clues were there? This is not as difficult as it seems, although it requires careful observation.

Using texts in Urdu, Punjabi Gujerati and Hindi will help children unfamiliar with these languages to recognise that there are considerable differences between scripts. Bilingual learners may be viewed as 'experts' and the spin-off may be a greater valuing of people who speak or write more then one language. Include languages such as Creoles which are more often spoken than written.

The *Word house* simulation game from *World studies 8-13* [9] focuses on the words which have become part of everyday usage in the English language which originate from other languages. *The languages book* [10] also suggests ideas for work in this area.

Oral tradition

It is not only individual words which travel, but also stories. These may travel over vast distances but are reminders of roots. Ananse stories from the Caribbean and Africa are obvious starting points, although most communities will have their own oral tradition. Parents and grandparents may be happy to tell stories to small groups. *Making stories* [11] is a practical resource book for looking at the oral tradition.

74

The people who came

The nature of many societies is that they are dynamic and ever changing. These changes come about for a wide variety of reasons. One major factor influencing change can be the communities and people who come as settlers, invaders, visitors, etc.

When studying groups of people who have come to this or to any other society, these questions offer a useful framework for discussions and children's research. They ensure that finding out about the Romans coming to Britain, for example, has a clear focus. The questions also offer a framework for connecting and comparing the experiences of different groups coming to one place over the centuries.

In the context of the national curriculum, children could look at groups like the Romans, Anglo-Saxons and Vikings, the black settlers who came in Tudor times, the immigration in Victorian Britain, the more recent immigration of people from Poland, Africa, the Indian sub continent, the Caribbean, Vietnam etc.

- **Who were they?** [What were their roots? Where were they from? What was life like at home?]

- **Why did they come?** [To find new land? To get jobs? Out of curiosity? etc.]

- **Who came and who was left behind?** [Did the men travel and the women stay at home? If so why?]

- **What was the encounter like when they arrived?** [Were they welcomed or resisted? Did they experience prejudice?]

- **What did they bring with them?** [A new language, technology, stories, architecture, slavery etc.]

- **How did they influence the society they came to?** [Are there lasting effects? Have they stayed and made the new country their home? Are there lasting benefits or problems?]

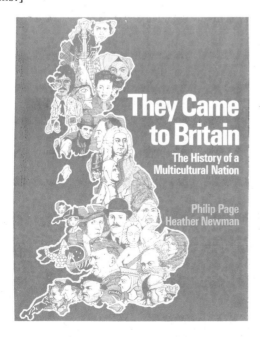

MOTHERLAND
West Indian Women to Britain in the 1950s

Elyse Dodgson

Racism

It is important that children understand that immigration is a present day experience as well an historical one. Some of the children may themselves have been born in another part of the world and may have memories of growing up there. Others may have parents and grandparents who have come to live in this country in their adult lives and will have stories and memories both of the place they grew up and also their arrival and reception in this country. It is likely that many of those experiences will have been painful ones in which incomers have encountered prejudice and racism. This is an important issue to address with children but needs to be handled sensitively.

Motherland†

Motherland is a resource which teachers have found useful for looking at recent immigration. It records the migration experiences of a number of women from the West Indies in their own words; their expectations when they came and the disappointment they felt on arrival. It covers issues such as first impressions, child care, work and housing.

Having set the scene about recent immigration, ask the children to imagine what a group of young women from the Caribbean would have felt when they came to Britain. Give some of the brief quotations to groups and ask them pick out the key words which describe how the women actually felt.

- Did they predict correctly?
- What were their own predictions based on?
- Why do they think the women felt disappointment?
- Do they think all people felt disappointed?
- What do they think those women feel like now, having lived here for many years?

Stories

Stories are an excellent medium for exploring issues of roots and journeys. Through fantasy, children can begin to imagine what it's like to be in someone else's shoes. These are example of stories you could use.

Not so fast Songololo, Niki Daly, Gollancz, 1985.
A delightful picture book set in South Africa about a young black boy who accompanies his grandmother on a shopping trip to the city. 5-8 yrs.

Angry river, Ruskin Bond, Methuen, 1972.
Sita, a young girl lives with her grandparents in India. She has to cope alone when the river floods and her island home is swept away. 6-9 years.

I am David, Anne Holm, Methuen, 1965.
David ,who has known no other life than the concentration camp, escapes into a world he knows nothing of. He takes a long perilous journey across Europe to a new country, but gradually begins to feel that there is hope and a real future waiting for him. A compassionate, powerful and moving book for older juniors.

Little brother, Allan Baillie, Blackie, 1985.
Eleven year old Vitny escapes to Thailand from Cambodia during the war, in search of his only surviving relative, his brother Mang. 10 plus

Journey to Jo'burg, Beverly Naidoo, Longman, 1985.
Naledi's and Tiro's mother works as a servant in Johannesburg; the children's journey to fetch her when their sister becomes ill forms the plot of this excellent book. 9-13 years.

When Hitler stole pink rabbit, Judith Kerr, Fontana, 1971.
The story of a German Jewish family in 1933 who leave home secretly under threat of death. Through the eyes of nine year old Anna, issues of being uprooted and continually having to function in a foreign language in a strange situation are explored. 10 plus.

The silver sword, Ian Serraillier, Puffin books 1970.
This is the story about the journey of a group of children from post second world war refugee camps to find their parents. 8-13 years

Moving, Meguido Zola, Hamish Hamilton, 1983.
A Hutterite colony living on the prairies of Canada early this century grows too large and certain families are chosen to move and found a new colony. It gently raises questions of choices in what communities cling to and what they leave behind. 6-9 years.

Ostrich egg - shell canteen, Musa Nagenda, Heinemann, 1973.
Set among the Bushmen of the Kalahari, the story follows the adventures of Khuana who want to acquire men's hunting skills. She and her grandmother end up abandoned and in grave danger and must make their journey alone to the next water-hole. 9-13 years.

Jyoti's journey, Helen Ganly, Andre Deutsch, 1986.
A story book about Jyoti's experience of immigration. Her father lives in Britain but Jyoti and the rest of her family live in India. In India we see her going to a cousin's wedding and preparing to come to England. India is shown as bright and colourful which contrasts sharply with Jyoti's first impressions of England as grey and cold.

Uprooted!

Many people have the experience of uprooting and moving to live in another part of the world. These activities are designed to raise issues about what we value ultimately and also about the circumstances in which people leave their homes.

'If someone told you that you had to leave the house in five minutes time, that you were leaving the country for ever, and that you could only take with you a plastic carrier bag, what would you put in it?'

Some people have to leave home at very short notice, collecting together their most important possessions. Out of this activity, you may be able to draw out what things are of most value to the children. You could ask them to bring in a bag of what they would take with them if they had to leave their home in a hurry. They could in pairs explain their choices.

What is most important to the children? Is there any overall pattern in the class? You may find that photographs and items of 'sentimental' value are more important than more costly goods.

To take this a step further, tell the children that there is a restriction on the weight they can can take and the items they have chosen are too heavy. They have to jettison excess weight. This can serve as a useful weighing activity. Ask the children to imagine who might be in this situation of having to leave home in a great hurry. You might get answers like people on the run from the police, people forced to leave the country for something they have done or believe in.

Refugees

If it has not already arisen, introduce the idea of refugees. Talk about different kinds of refugees e.g those who are refugees because of their political/religious beliefs or because of their economic status. Save the Children Fund has produced a primary school resource pack called *Refugees*† which offers useful case studies and practical ideas for exploring the experiences further.

The stories opposite illustrate the potential for exploring issues through fiction; many look at the experience of refugees. What is it like going to a new place? Are refugees welcomed or treated with suspicion? Use evidence such as newspaper articles for these discussions.

School assemblies can be used to enhance themes. One school where all the classes took the theme of journeys had a series of assemblies featuring the experiences of refugees.

Diaries

Because diaries focus on feelings about an experience rather than just a record of what happens, they can be a valuable tool for building up an understanding of issues. They can also be a popular format for children's own writing. One class of children were reading *Journey to Jo'burg* [see opposite] and at various points role played* the story. Having talked about how they felt about it, they then wrote a diary to record their feelings. Children could also have a go at writing accounts from different perspectives. In *Journey to Jo'burg*, how might the two children, the mother, the police, the mother's employer each see the situation?

The painting *'The last of England'* by Ford Madox Brown, depicts a young couple about to set sail for Australia and a new life. A diary of the journey; the leaving, the sailing and how they might have been received in the new land would offer much scope for work. Other paintings at your local art gallery can offer valuable starting points.

The story of Mary Seacole also offers great potential for diary writing. Mary Seacole, a nurse from Jamaica ended up working in the army hospital in the Crimean War. She met with tremendous resistance in her quest to use her nursing skills, partly because she was a woman and probably also because she was black. She has never gained the same recognition as her counterpart Florence Nightingale.

The Last of England by Ford Madox Brown, in the City of Birmingham Museum and Art Gallery.

Resources: Roots and journeys

A balloon for grandad, Nigel Gray, Orchard Books, 1988.
Sam's balloon flies off over mountains, sea and deserts until it reaches his grandad Abdulla sitting under the mango tree. The story of a balloon's journey.

Books to break barriers, a review guide to multicultural fiction 4-18, Oxford DEC, 1986.
An invaluable resource for every teacher interested in using stories to explore issues, concepts or themes.

Borderlines; Uprooted; Four stories, Christian Aid, 1984.
Christian Aid has produced some excellent, leaflets on the theme of exiles and migration. *Borderlines* is a five minute board game to help children understand some of the hazards of escaping from civil war to safety. *Uprooted* is notes for teachers based on the stories of moving of four children from around the world.

Black settlers in Britain 1555 to 1958, Nigel File and Chris Power, Heinemann Educational books, 1981.
Black people have been in Britain for a long time. This book charts their presence using facsmile documents, newspaper extracts, painting and photographs. An excellent source book for this theme.

Mary Seacole, nursing heroine, MGSS Coventry, 1986.
The story of Mary Seacole a black nurse in the Crimean War, in the form of overhead projector transparencies. The original tale is available with some editorial comments as *Wonderful adventures of Mrs Seacole in many lands*, Ziggi Alexander and Audrey Dewjee, Falling Wall Press, 1857/1984.

Motherland, West Indian Women in the 1950's, Elyse Dodgson, 1984.
In the 1950's thousands of people left the West Indies for Britain. Many were women who left friends, family and children behind. This books explores the experiences of the women involved, through quotations and stories. Devised as part of a project by pupils of Vauxhall Manor School, many of them daughters of migrant women.

The people who came, books 1-3, Longman Caribbean, 1970.
Three secondary text books which trace the history of people who travelled to and settled in the Caribbean. Written in narrative style, they form useful background for teachers, with ideas that can be adapted for use with younger children.

Profile on prejudice, Nikki van der Gaag and Lynne Gerlach, Minority Rights Group, 1985.
A pack aimed at older students which engages people's feelings when working at minority experiences. A simulation game looks at the experiences of Native Americans, Travellers and Palestinians. A simplified version could be used with younger children.

Refugees, a primary school resource, Save the Children Fund, 1988.
A topic pack designed to help primary children understand the concept of 'refugees' whilst also challenging negative stereotypes. The activities are practical and well explained; the pack also contains photographs and case studies of individuals who have experiences as refugees.

Roots and shoots, a schools garden project, Oxford D.E. Unit, 1988.
This book describes how four schools set up their own school gardens. There is a clear science base to the work - observing the life cycle of plants, the effects of water and light etc. Correspondence to exchange experiences, was set up with overseas schools running their own garden projects.

Teaching and learning about refugees resources list, British Refugee Council 1989, available from BRC, Bondway House, 3/9 Bondway, London, SW8 1SJ.
An excellent overview of resources for work on refugees, both for teachers and children.

They came to Britain, the history of a multicultural nation, Philip Page and Heather Newman, Edward Arnold, 1985.
Although designed for secondary students, this acts as a useful source book on peoples who have come to Britain.

We are Mesquakie, we are one, Hadley Irwin, Sheba, 1984.
An exciting story which tells the experience of the Mesquakie people through the eyes of a young girl. The reader is left with a powerful image of Mesquakie culture and their reactions to white settlers who encroach on their lifestyle. For older juniors - or can be read and paraphrased by the teacher.

Worlds of difference, Esther Bisset and Martin Palmer, WWF/Blackie, 1985.
This book examines how eight religions or belief systems tell about how and why the world began. These creation stories shown how the people understand their world. Activities to ascertain meanings of these stories are also suggested in an accompanying booklet.

Images

Holiday snapshot
It was certainly one
for the holiday album;
a postcard advertisement
for coca-cola and rum.
A palm-fringed bay
with yachts of prosperity
tacking in the breeze;
the dollar buoyant;

while everywhere
that smell of affluence
- sweat and sun-tan lotion -
rising off bodies

pinking in the sun
like lobsters on a spit.
A postcard advertisement
for coca-cola and rum.

No camera recorded
the sharks of greed;
the weed of deception
a deceit beneath surfaces.

There was no indication
of the martial fist
that composed this picture
to lure the tourist.

It was certainly one
for the holiday album
a postcard advertisement
for coca-cola and rum.

Cecil Rajendra, *taken from Dove on fire [1]*

Images play a vital role in the way we learn about the world. The role of images is particularly important when we are learning about the unfamiliar, as a single powerful image can 'freeze' our ideas about another person or place. Classroom work on images can help children understand that people may perceive situations differently and that these perceptions may be based on little information. This theme offers suggestions for enabling children to develop skills in questioning, judging, debating etc. so that they can explore and question their own attitudes and perceptions.

In the national curriculum:
There are many ways of developing a theme around *Images* in the context of national curriculum. In activities set out in this section, we have chosen to focus on the potential for English, science, geography and history. There are many opportunities for making the focus of the theme another curriculum area. The web on page 83 illustrates some of the questions raised by the theme in this book. These are by no means exhaustive.

The theme draws on the English ATs 1, 2 and 3 for speaking and listening, reading and writing. Media education forms a main focus for children learning particularly through the use of photographs, newspapers and advertisements. Opportunities for using story and drama are also suggested.

Images draws on a number of geographical skills and concepts. Suggestions are made for finding information from secondary sources; for local area geography work; for drawing links between the locality and the wider world; for children to explore their own perceptions, their likes and dislikes about places. Suggestions are made for preparing for field work and discussing issues about protecting the environment.

As with the geographical work on the local area, there is potential for exploring children's images of life in the past. This would fit well into a school designed history study unit on local history. Many opportunities arise for scientific investigations around AT15 using light. The skills set out in AT1 will enable open ended explorations.

In order to develop a deeper understanding of the world around us, it is important to bring our attitudes and images into the open. This section explores some ways of doing this.

Images of the wider world

The way in which we see things is affected by our preconceived images and ideas. Not surprisingly, there are some things about which people tend to have similar images. This may be because our images are influenced by powerful sources such as television, books and advertisements. Sometimes they will reinforce or create one type of image - if this image is presented at the expense of all others, it can become a stereotype.

For instance, adverts for peanuts, Blue Peter safaris, Tarzan films and nature programmes may all feed into the image that Africa only consists of jungle, deserts and wild animals. There may be some truth in the image portrayed, however these images do not reflect the whole truth, nor the idea that there are facets which are totally ignored.

We also need to recognise that powerful images can be created by the media. For most children, television is the major source of images of the wider world. Before the Falklands war, few British school children would have any knowledge or image of Argentinians, but within days of the 'Task Force' being sent, children were playing 'Brits v Argies' in playgrounds around the country and many had developed a strong image of Argentinians as the evil enemy.

City life, rural life

If children have images which they consider to be negative, these can often hinder a real understanding of a situation and can block an ability to build up empathy. On the other hand, if they perceive their images to be positive, these may create curiosity or encourage interest in learning. Whether these are 'positive' or 'negative', if their understanding remains narrow or over simplistic, then these images are blocking a deeper awareness of the subject in question.

For instance, if children consider they have a 'positive' image of Kenya because they think it is full of lions and elephants, this may spur their interest in learning about Kenya. If however, this image is not challenged or broadened, the children are likely to have a limited view of life in Kenya.

People associate positive images with city life and negative images with rural living. It is easy to see the roots of this argument, in the fact that city life may offer more similarities with life in [urban parts of] Britain. However it is built on a false premise that city life is necessarily better than rural life. The real challenge lies in helping children to appreciate the value of a range of lifestyles, including those which seem very different from their own, without reinforcing a 'noble savage' image.

Images and values

Children begin to piece together a mental map of the world at an early age. Michael Storm discusses the role of images in more detail in his article *Children's images of other countries - the influence of the media* [2]. He refers to research carried out by Jahoda and Tajfel which explored children's attitudes to other countries. They found that 'emotional attitudes to various foreign countries crystallize earlier than the assimilation of even the most rudimentary factual knowledge about them'. Children would not just develop a stereotype of a particular group but they were likely to be able to label that group as *'goodies'* or *'baddies'*. This is reflected in contemporary children's cartoons, such as Action Force and Defenders of the Earth where beauty is often equated with goodness and ugliness with evil.

Michael Storm argues that although children may have formed images of other groups at this age, they are also very curious about other people and flexible in their attitudes.

UNESCO research [2] in 1967 showed that children reach a peak of friendliness to foreigners at the age of about ten. At this age they are most tolerant of other people and most able to consider others as similar to themselves. They are more ready to like people who seem different from themselves.

If children are most flexible and open in their attitudes in the primary school, then this is an ideal time to help them to recognise and challenge their own images. Building up skills in doing this can help children to continue to question the images they have.

Recent research by Susan Lynn and Janet Graham [3] explores how children view photographs of the countries of the South. It was clear from their findings that a great deal of work needs to be done with primary children on reading visual images of unfamiliar places in order to counteract the stereotypes which are often created.

Images we present

Some of the issues behind the images which we present to children are explored here.

Walk into the average primary classroom and you will be bombarded by a variety of visual images, some created by the children, others from books, posters and displays. The visual image is exploited by most teachers to create a stimulating atmosphere for learning.

However, there are images that are rarely seen in primary classrooms; their absence can give powerful messages about what is the norm and what is acceptable. One teacher told how two very quiet Vietnamese children in her class would not respond very much. When she brought in a book about a Vietnamese child, they suddenly became very excited and had a lot to talk about because they could identify with the child in the book; their 'home' experience was being recognised at school.

Another teacher took photographs of his pupils and used them for discussion; some were cut up and made into booklets or puppets. When images of yourself and your friends are used as everyday resources in school, this acts as a tremendous boost for children, both in terms of their own self image and their confidence.

As well as representing familiar experiences, it is also important to introduce new ones. No class will reflect the diversity of Britain's multi-ethnic society, nor will it reflect the variety of lifestyles around the world. Images of the wider world need to permeate classroom life. These may include music, artefacts, people, food as well as pictures; a multi sensory approach may help create a fairer perspective.

Positive and negative

Amongst some teachers, there is a wide concern that children should be presented with positive images of black people, particularly those who live in the countries of the South. This arises out of the concern that some of the images particularly of people are derogatory or patronising. Other images are completely omitted.

It is important that children see black people in positive roles and situations. Most of the pictures children see of the countries of the South tend to be of starving children or helpless adults. Although these situations exist, we tend not to see people taking responsibility for their lives and making their own decisions. Children need to see these 'positive' images and understand that these are real situations. They also need to develop the wisdom to question negative imagery. What are the reasons underlying such poverty?

We must be careful not to see 'positive' and 'negative' images in too simplistic a way. The following extract from the magazine *Issues in race and education* [4] describes the results of an activity which involved teachers selecting a series of images to accompany a given text. The text was about racism in Britain and the images chosen fell into two broadly different categories.

> '*The first which could typify a multicultural response involved rejecting images considered to be 'negative' (street violence, 'threatening' black youth) and focusing on 'positive' images of interracial harmony and co-operation (black and white children at play, a racially mixed football team). Here again, the question to be asked is: 'positive for whom?' A shot of a relatively affluent black couple may be 'positive' in so far as it suggests that there is a black middle-class which is reaping material rewards: yet if this is not accompanied by a recognition of continuing inequalities in housing, employment and wealth, then it is clearly 'positive' only in a very limited sense. One has only to look at the South African equivalent of 'Ebony', with its glossy image of wealthy black people, to realise the dangers of such an approach.*
>
> *The second type of response, which is at least potentially anti-racist, relies on exposing the contradictions within and between images, by juxtaposing images which give radically different impressions of blacks and whites in British society. In one startling instance, a group used images which subverted the complacent assumptions of the commentary. To accompany a piece of text which read 'a Welshman, an Irishman, a Scotsman and an Englishman' were a series of images of an Asian shopkeeper, a young black man, a black bus conductor and a young black woman. The national stereotypes and the male bias of the commentary were directly confronted.*'

You could use this extract with colleagues to think about the images you present in the classroom. Does this challenge you about the pictures you display? Are there points with which you agree or disagree?

Distant but familiar?

A commitment to child centred education has often led to a linear approach to learning, starting with the child, moving out to the locality, then onto the country and the wider world. Although this is a valid approach in some situations, it is not without its difficulties. We need to be careful not to confirm children's notions that the distant is different.

Choosing images

If we follow this traditional pattern when using photographs and concentrate on using those taken only in local or very similar situations we may be denying children's experience and knowledge as well as limiting exposure to new situations. This can be compounded, if when we do use photographs of other places they are treated as something different or unusual.

We may find that children are able to relate more easily to a photograph taken in another part of the world then one taken closer to home. Geographical setting is no indication of familiarity. An image of Islamabad market may be more familiar to the children than that of yachting on the Isle of Wight either because they have travelled to Pakistan, or because they know markets in other parts of the world, or because they regularly go to their own local market.

Equally, an image of children playing in the street in Vietnam may be familiar to the children because they can relate to the idea of children playing. The similarity of the activity may override the difference of locality.

We cannot always assume that the local is always easy to relate to, for example an image of local housing which is very different from that in which the children live may seem strange.

Through television children are daily exposed to images from many parts of the world. If we only select images of the local situation to use in the classroom we may be in danger of creating false distinctions in children's minds. Constant use of images from a range of situations can help counteract any false distinctions.

Where can I get such images from?
There are many sources of images of other parts of the world which you can use effectively with children. These are a few starting points:

Published photopacks see page 86.

The New Internationalist calendar, twelve striking images of life in different parts of the world with useful background information in visual form for teachers.

Calendars, the children may receive gifts of calendars from relatives and friends in other countries. There are sometimes free gifts of calendars from restaurants at Christmas time.

Desk diaries, especially those from UNICEF and OXFAM.

Posters especially those from Christian Aid, OXFAM, ACER.

Newspapers, colour supplements, postcards, magazines.

Overseas magazines from churches [many of these show a range of images much broader than the traditional missionary outside a church].

Addresses can be found on page 111.

what influences your images?

do you think this is a true picture?

what images do you have of other places like Brazil or Barbados?

how do you see your family, your friend, t.v. stars etc.?

if so, how?

do you want to change your image?

how do you feel about it?

can you draw a picture or mental map of it?

how do others see you?

is this a fair picture?

how do you see yourself?

how do you see the place where you live?

Images

who might create an image?

can you create headlines to go with a picture to show different viewpoints?

can you design and make your own camera?

can you create your own photographs without a camera?

can you represent a person or a place using different words and pictures?

can you take your own photographs?

can you investigate the part which light plays in making photographs?

how are different groups represented in newspapers e.g. old people?

can you enlarge photographs using scale drawings?

does the camera ever lie?

can you collect evidence for this?

does a photograph tell the whole story?

is it fair representation?

The theme: Images

As it is often difficult to recognise the images we hold, it is useful to begin by questioning images of people and places with which we are familiar. The understandings which we develop can be used as a basis for looking at images of the unfamiliar.

Images of people

As a way of introducing the concept of images, it is useful to start with something concrete such as images of ourselves and other people.

Labels - how do you see yourself?

Draw a picture of yourself in the centre of a sheet of paper, with labels attached to it. Then think of some words which describe yourself and put one in each label. It might help if the class brainstormed* a list of possible words first. Get together in pairs and explain why you have chosen the words. Would others describe you in the same way?

The children could build on this by writing a description of themselves and then asking one of their friends to see if they would agree with it or have written it the same way. Bilingual children speaking the same language could work together and if able record their labels in dual scripts.

This type of activity can be successfully utilised in profiling. If done at regular intervals, it could give an interesting picture of emotional and attitudinal development to balance more academic indicators.

Viewpoints

Children could think about how others see them. Fill in sentences such as the following:

My mum thinks I am....................
My brother thinks I am...............
My sister thinks I am...................
My teacher thinks I am...............

Develop this by writing a series of short paragraphs about yourself as if they were written by different people. How about writing your own school report or a letter from your mum to a relative describing what sort of things you are doing at the moment? What images do people have of you? Are they a true reflection? If you write a description of yourself anonymously, can your friends guess who it is?

Images of Inuits

Build on this by using images of people the children do not know and ask them to imagine how other people might see them. Include images of people in different settings, in a range of geographical or historical contexts. Use the viewpoints activity , so, if you have a picture of an Inuit [sometimes called an Eskimo]   fill in these sentences:

His mum thinks he is....................
His sister thinks he is...................
His friend thinks he is.................
I think he is..................................
He thinks he is.............................

OHOVELUK

In this context it would be useful to use books such as the *Beans* [5] series in which children from different parts of the world speak about themselves and their lives. In this case would be very useful in challenging over simplistic views.

The activities designed to be used with faces in the *Change* theme can be adapted to explore images of people.

My grandma has black hair†

Stories can be a useful stimulus for discussing our images of people. Tell the children that you are going to read them a story of a girl's grandmother and the kinds of things she does. In pairs, ask them to write down what sorts of things they think will come up in the story and draw what the grandma looks like. Read the story and afterwards discuss reactions. The grandma in the story is quite different from those usually found in books and challenges images of older people. You could try a similar activity with other books which challenge stereotypes of any sort.

'Consequences'

Sit in a circle in a group of six, each person with a pen and A4 sheet of paper. Everyone should write their name at the bottom of the sheet. The aim of the activity is to collect six positive statements about yourself by playing 'consequences'. First, each person should write a positive statement about herself at the top of the page and fold it over so no-one can see. All pass it on and write a positive statement about the person whose name is at the base of the page. Pass it on again until it gets back to the start, then read the results.

How do you see yourself?

chatterbox

funny

giggly

naughty

clever

I like books

nosey

A place you know...the school

It is useful to look at an experience or place which all the children know about; the school itself offers an ideal focus. The fact that there will be different views makes it a good way of exploring images.

A school brochure
One way of finding out how children see the school is to ask them to make a brochure about it which includes a variety of photographs or drawings. The brochure must be fairly small, so only a limited number of pictures can be used.

Groups could brainstorm* first which pictures they might include. Out of this list, the group then decide on a limited number, which give a general overall view of the school, thinking carefully about the captions for the pictures and the information used. These images could be drawn or photographed. If the children are going to take photographs themselves, some useful strategies for this can be found in *Get the Picture!* †.

Groups could compare their brochures and see if they have presented similar images. Do the brochures say anything about the people who compiled them? Groups could be asked, in secret, to produce brochures for different purposes, e.g. to encourage certain groups to send their children to the school, to show that the school is particularly interested in sport, etc. The rest of the class could guess who the brochure is aimed at.

Schools are now publishing their own brochures; how do the children's brochures compare with the school's own?

How the school works
Draw, individually or in groups of three or four, two pictures of your school, one depicting the school working well, the other, the school working badly. List the differences between the two pictures and try to identify what makes a good school.

Use the photographs from the *Behind the scenes*† pack, asking children to sort them into two piles, one of schools they would like to go to and the other of schools they would not like to go to. This could lead into a discussion about what the children dislike about their school and how they might go about improving it.

Mental maps*
Imagine there is a new child in the class. You have each been given the responsibility of drawing a map to show her how to get round the school. First, draw a map between your classroom and the dining room, showing the important places that you pass. When you have finished, compare your results.

How do you think a caretaker or teacher might have drawn the same area? What does this say about your images of the school?

Behind the Scenes

Positive/negative booklets
One teacher wanted to explore the idea that words can alter the meaning of a picture. She took a group of children round the school, taking two photographs at key points in the building. The children then made a booklet using one of each pair and wrote positive comments under each picture. With the remainder of the photographs, they made another booklet but this time writing negative comments. The comments under the photograph of bare display boards were:

> **positive**
> a new term gives us a chance to fill the boards with interesting displays of this term's work;
> **negative**
> people do not care about how the school looks, no-one bothers to put anything on the display boards.

These booklets created a lot of discussion and stimulated the children to make their own booklets and produce biased scripts.

Using the same idea, try writing a positive/negative booklet for a set of photographs for a place which the children do not know, e.g. for a set of images from a calendar of Australia, or for a series of images in a Sunday supplement.

Write your own text!
Block out the text from a double page spread in a book which shows life in another part of the world and ask the children to write two different texts to go with the pictures, a positive and a negative one. What did they write? Which did they find easier to write and why do they think this was? How does what they wrote compare with the real text? What did they think of the real text?

Picturing your place

Children will have some common experience of the local community. These activities build on this experience for developing geographical and historical concepts and skills.

A mental map*

Tell the children that someone has recently moved into their road. Ask them to draw a map which explains to the new person the different places they play in or use, e.g. the manhole cover where they play marbles, the road where they play football, where the ice cream van stops etc. Which places do children have a special familiarity with? Which do they feel are 'their' territory? How do they feel if someone else 'trespasses' on 'their' space? Are there spaces or places that they feel frightened of? This is an opportunity to help children recognise their own attitudes to their local area.

Five places

Brainstorm* a list of things you can see when you walk round your local community, e.g. the sweet shop or the canal. Go for a walk and see how much you remember when you get back. If you had to show a visitor around the area and only had time to visit ten places, which ten would they think would be most interesting? Does this tell you anything about how you see your local area? Are there any great differences of opinion?

If there is a calendar of your local area, what other photos would you add to it to make it a more realistic view? Which of the pictures would you remove? Look at other calendars of Britain and see what you would add or take away.

In the past...

If the people who had lived in your area thirty years ago had to do the same thing, what might they have chosen? If you can invite two or three such people to each give you their five images. Do these give different views of the past? This also offers a basis for discussing different perceptions over time as well as space.

Painting

Ask the children to paint a picture of their own place. The use of colour can often reflect more subtle attitudes. We asked some children from different schools to paint pictures of their own area. These were some of the observations some of their teachers made when discussing the images the children had created. The activity gave the teachers an insight into how their children understood their own place, as well as being important for the children to clarify their own ideas.

You could develop this by then asking the children to paint pictures of places with which they are less familiar. These could be places in the news. Follow up by discussing why they depicted the place as they did and where their images might have come from.

Over half the children were impressed by the amenities in the area. Everything they needed was there – and that is what they drew. About half also represented fighting, graffiti and vandalism in their pictures...

The children in Handsworth seemed to have a much stronger and more positive view of their place than the children in Kingstanding. When the children in Kingstanding drew their images, some of them drew the centre of Birmingham, the bullring, telecom tower and Central TV...

The children drew the things they knew about St Albans; some thought the seaside was there. They found it very difficult to put boundaries on the place they live. They also didn't have any idea about what people's perceptions about St Albans might be....

Materials for work on images

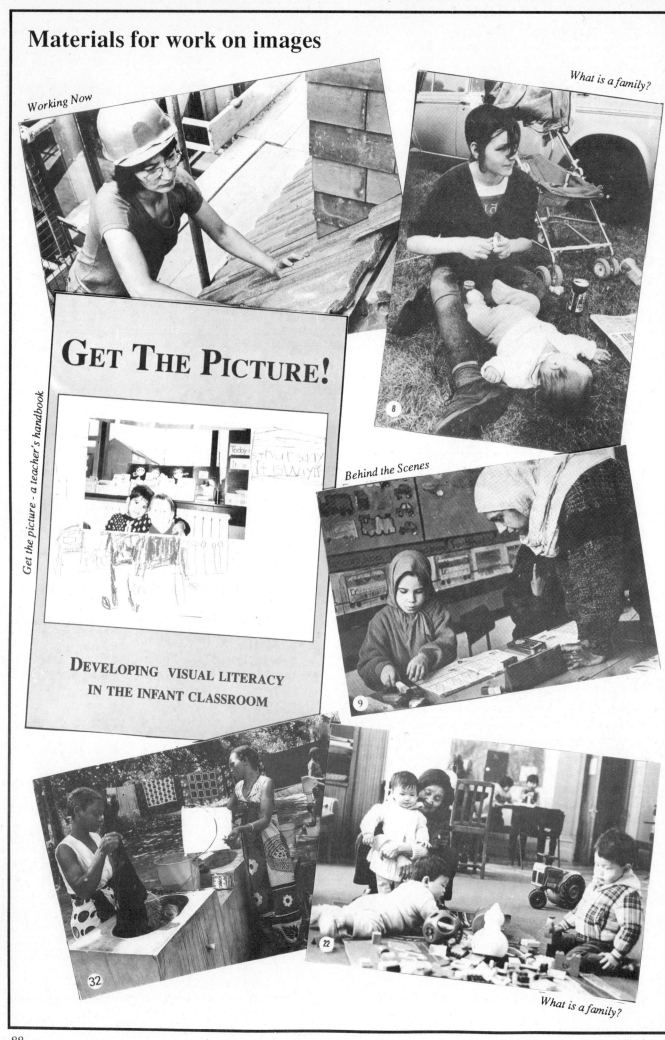

Working Now

What is a family?

8

Get the picture - a teacher's handbook

GET THE PICTURE!

DEVELOPING VISUAL LITERACY
IN THE INFANT CLASSROOM

Behind the Scenes

9

32

22

What is a family?

In the papers

Newspapers are an ideal, cheap resource for discussing the images we receive of our own society and other places.

Using photographs

Photographs of the local community are a useful stimulus for discussing images. The photograph activities on pages 42 to 46 can be used along with the ideas outlined below to bring out children's perceptions of their own area. Published packs such as *City images*† which contain photographs of Birmingham are useful resources.

Compile your own set by selecting photographs or postcards of your own area. Run off a film of the locality or get the children to take their own photographs. *Get the Picture!*† shows how a group of 6 year olds took photographs to illustrate their walk to school.

To develop map work skills, pin a large map of your local area on the wall and see if the children can locate the places where the photographs were taken.

Headlines

Ask groups to choose one photograph and imagine it is on the front page of the local paper. Make a headline for that photograph. When each group has made a headline and shared it with the rest of the class, ask them to go back into their groups with the same photograph and brainstorm* as many headlines for that photograph as they can. This might bring out the very different ways we might 'read' a photograph and show that even in one picture we can see many different images.

Give each group of children the same selection of headlines. Display a set of photographs of your area and make sure each one is clearly numbered. The children could use their own selection cut out of papers. Include national papers with international news coverage. Ask the children to look closely at the photographs and the headlines and then to decide which headlines go best with which photographs. When the group has decided, they should make a list putting the number of the appropriate photograph next to the headline.

Counting the images

How often do pictures of black people appear in newspapers? Do they tend to be found in certain parts of the paper, or in relation to certain stories? This activity is an opportunity for children to do some research into this area.

Before the children start, ask them to predict what they expect to find. Do they expect to find an equal number of black and white people? Do they expect to find them spread evenly throughout the paper?

Each group will need a newspaper and a large felt tipped pen. Ask them to go through the paper systematically and highlight the pictures of black people with their pen. Then they need to go back and record in an appropriate way, on what pages the images were found and in relation to which stories. Data can then be collated in a graph or pie chart to be shared with the rest of the class.

It is generally still the case that the majority of pictures of black people fall on the sports pages or appear with crime stories. It is very important to debrief this activity carefully, so that children discuss possible reasons for the distribution of images which they have found or the absence of them. You will need to discuss whether the children think this is a true representation of black people's newsworthy achievements. The children could think about alternative images which they would like to see of black people; photographs from a number of photopacks could be used to illustrate this.

City Images

Give examples of some of the achievements of black people which rarely get coverage. The *Black makers of history series*, includes titles such as *Four women; The real McCoy, an A-Z of black people in science and technology* and *Not just singin' and dancin', black people in the arts*†.

Variations on a theme

Try the same activity with images of older people, disabled people, images of family life etc. Try a similar activity counting how often other parts of the world are recorded in the news. Which countries are referred to most over the period of one week? Does this vary from newspaper to newspaper?

Somewhere new?

Suggestions are made for exploring images of unfamiliar situations.

Before a visit

Preparation for a school visit has great potential for exploring images of the unfamiliar because it is possible to discuss the differences between the images children hold prior to the visit and what is actually experienced.

Before the class visits a place, ask them to think about what they expect to find there. Record this in the form of a short piece of writing, in a mental map* of the place or in a series of words. Where do they think their images have come from? Whilst on the visit, the children could note the things that surprise them, things they did not expect to see and also things which fulfil their expectations.

After the visit, refer back to their pre-visit images. Were they fulfilled or challenged by the visit? This might begin to show how images do not always match up to reality. Did the children come away with different images of the same place?

Tourism

Tourist literature and advertising can influence children's images of places they do not know. Because these materials usually portray very limited images, it is important that they are used in a critical way to help children explore the ideas behind them.

In pairs, think about what makes a place good for a holiday; make a list of some important criteria. Next, select the three most important things which would attract you to a place. Is there a general consensus of ideas amongst the class? How do people choose where they go on holiday? [It may be better to talk about this in general terms, particularly if some children do not have the opportunity for a holiday.]

Replies like the following might be given:

* *Somewhere recommended by a friend or relative;*
* *By looking at brochures or guidebooks;*
* *Television adverts;*
* *Where we've been before;*
* *Somewhere we can afford.*

Are the children or their parents influenced by TV adverts or brochures? What attracts them to one holiday rather than another?

A brochure survey

Give each group of children a selection of tourist brochures. Ask them to go through the brochure tallying the number of times similar images appear, e.g. the swimming pool, the beach, local traditional events. Which of these may or may not attract tourists? Are there any common findings? What does this say about the images presented in brochures?

See pages 106 and 107 for further suggestions for work on tourism.

Similar pictures

To illustrate that there are similarities between different parts of the world, show the children a series of pictures of cities and ask them to guess where they are. Cities such as San Paolo, Nairobi, Calcutta can all look much the same as London, Manchester and Birmingham. Display these photographs around a world map and ask them to guess in which parts of the world they were taken.

The World Wide Fund for Nature has produced a set of similar photographs of life in Calcutta and London called *A tale of two cities*†. These would serve as an excellent stimulus for this activity.

A variety of pictures

One way of helping children build up the concept that there is tremendous diversity within any country, is to select a variety of pictures and ask the children to guess where they were taken. The photographs on the page opposite were all taken in The Gambia and Senegal in West Africa, within two hundred miles of each other. They look as if they could have been almost anywhere in the world.

Give each group of children a photocopy of the page and ask them to say where they think each of the photos was taken. Don't tell them that they were all taken in one area. Another way of using them would be to ask the children which photos they think were taken in the same country and give their reasons.

When you debrief the discussion, it would be in interesting to see if the children recognised any of the photographs as Africa.

The locations of the photographs:

A Basse, The Gambia;
B St Louis, Senegal;
C Brikama, The Gambia;
D Dakar railway station, Senegal;
E Dakar, Senegal;
F Goree island, Senegal.

Where do you think these photographs were taken?

A

B

C

D

E

A LA VIERGE MARIE MERE DE JESUS LE SAUV

F

Making images

Images are created for specific reasons. The ideas on this page illustrate how you might introduce the concept of the created image.

Photography is both an artform and a science. This theme offers a context for exploring both dimensions of photography. It is well worth referring to the *Manual for classroom photography†*.

Children can make their own pictures using light sensitive paper. This first involves collecting objects which will let some light through, e.g. flowers, leaves, feathers etc. Arrange these on a sheet of light sensitive paper, then place a piece of glass or perspex over them to keep the objects in place. Leave this in the sunlight for anything from 20 seconds to 30 minutes, depending on the strength of the sun. Finally submerge the paper in a tray of fixer, according to the time set out in the instructions and then wash thoroughly with water. The design should be clear on the paper.

Photograms
Photograms can be made using similar principles. You will need a darkroom or a walk in cupboard which can be blacked out. Instead of using objects which let light through, this time the children should choose opaque items e.g. a pencil, paper clips, unifix cubes, a comb, a pair of scissors. Arrange the objects on the light sensitive paper. Expose the design by switching on an anglepoise lamp 35-45 cm above it for two seconds. You can also use a torch. Submerge the paper in a tray of developer; rinse it and then in a tray of fixer and rinse it again.

With both these activities the children can experiment with different variables of time, objects, strength and sources of light. What happens to create images?

You can also explore how reflections are created and how images are distorted through using mirrors, as in the fairground. Maths work on symmetry and rotation also fit well into this theme.

Advertisements
Advertisements are a widely available resource which can be used with children to explore how images are created. Because they are designed to sell an item to a specific market, they use carefully selected words and pictures to create an appealing image. Look at fairly blatant examples and more subtle ones to explore how images distort the truth.

Personalities
Images are not only created around products, but also around people. Pop stars and royalty frequently have a following because of the image that is created of them. Why not look at one person who is often in the news to see the images created about them?

Voque activities
You can create a particular image by cropping photographs* so that only certain parts are shown. An example of this is shown opposite. This illustrates how an image can be cropped, to alter the information a picture gives. The girl in these pictures was refugee living in a drainpipe in the outskirts of Calcutta. She had fled from East Pakistan [now Bangladesh] during the border war of 1971. The drainpipes were standing on a swampy area which was awaiting drainage so that it could be used as a building site.

Photocopy the page opposite so that there is one sheet per group. Cut the three pictures out and give each group the first one. Ask them to answer these questions:
> *Where is the girl in the photograph?*
> *What is she doing?*
> *How do you think she is feeling?*

Feedback the groups' reactions.

Now give them the second photograph, with these questions:
> *Where is she sitting?*
> *What do you think she is looking at?*
> *How do you think she is feeling?*

Feedback the groups' reactions.

Give them the final picture with these questions:
> *Where is the photographs taken?*
> *What do you think is happening?*
> *How do you think the girl is feeling?*

In a final discussion, having told the children where the photograph was taken, you could talk about how their perceptions changed at different stages.

Other ideas for cropping activities can be found on page 46. The children can have a go themselves at cropping images for each other.

Resources: Images

Behind the scenes, photographs and inservice activities for exploring the hidden curriculum, DEC, 1988.
A photoset of the primary school e.g. the playground, dinner time, classrooms etc. Designed initially for teachers who are interested in looking at hidden curriculum issues, the photographs are also a useful resource to stimulate children talking about their own experience of school.

Beyond the frame - a pack of photographs and activities, English Language Resources Centre, Hampshire LEA, 1989.
20 A5 black and white photographs of children and adults designed to challenge issues of gender, race and disability.

Black makers of history series, Peckham Publishing Project, 1988 onwards. There are three titles so far in the series: *Four women; The real McCoy, an A-Z of black people in science and technology* and *Not just singin' and dancin', black people in the arts.*
Designed originally for adult basic education, these books have become very popular in schools because they supply information about black people in history which it is difficult to locate elsewhere, and the language is simple.

Us and the kids, resources for parent groups, DEC, 1991.
This colour photopack for use with parent groups, illustrates parents and children in everyday learning situations in different parts of the world.

City images, priorities for development, DEC, 1990.
A colour A4 photopack of images of the city of Birmingham. The photographs show life in the city centre, suburbs and inner city and can be used to form a wider context for exploring issues of family lifestyles.

Classroom photography, Carol Colledge, Ilford, 1984.
Available from Ilford, P.O. Box 21, Southall, Middlesex UB2 4AB.
A beautifully presented guide to classroom photography using simple materials. Each activity is set out in easy to follow steps and illustrated by example of children's work. Excellent for scientific investigations.

Doing things in and about the home, Trentham Books, 1983/7.
The photos show adults and children in traditional and non-traditional gender roles at home. The teachers' booklet is packed with ideas for using photographs in the primary classroom to raise gender issues.

Get the picture! developing visual literacy in the infant classroom, DEC, 1989.
A handbook to support teachers in developing young children's understanding of images. Strategies are included for using readily available images and photographs to raise issues about representation. Practical guidelines are also given for putting children behind the camera.

Moving on, a photopack on travellers in Britain, Minority Rights Group, 1987.
Travellers experience of misrepresentation in the media. This pack shows the richness and complexity of Travellers' lives and raises some of the issues facing Travelling communities in Britain.

My grandma has black hair, M. Hoffman and J. Burroughes, Beaver/Methuen, 1988.
Story book grannies have grey hair and sit knitting in their rocking chairs, but this gran is a hopeless knitter and rides around town in a noisy old car. For young children.

Tale of two cities - Calcutta and London, WWF, 1989.
54 black and white photographs which challenge our perceptions of life in these two cities. Similar themes such as transport, work, education, commerce etc. are addressed in each place. The juxtaposition of images raises issues about similarities and differences.

Water - photographs, case studies and activities, DEC, 1990.
A colour photopack raising issues about the use and availability of water in Africa. The teachers' notes are designed for use with upper secondary, but the photographs would be a very valuable stimulus for project looking at water in a global context with younger children.

What is a family? - photographs and activities, DEC, 1985, revised, 1990.
These 24 black and white photographs of families can be used to stimulate discussion about the children's ideas of family life. The teaching ideas in the accompanying booklet can be adapted for use in the primary school. A new set of photographs is now available.

Working now, photographs and activities for exploring gender roles in the primary classroom, DEC, 1989.
16 A4 black and white photographs of women and men in non-traditional working roles e.g. a male dancer, female mechanics and barristers. The teachers' handbook is full of practical activities for using the photographs and designing a whole scheme of work around them.

Change

Song of hope
At that hour
when the sun
slinks off
behind hills
and night
- a panther
crouches
ready to spring
upon our un-
suspecting city....

i want to sing
the coiled desires
of this land
the caged dreams
of forgotten men

i want to sing
of all that was
but no longer is
of all that
never was but
could have been

i want to sing
the obsidian
unspelled hopes
of our children
i want to sing
to remind us
never to despair
that every hour
every minute
somewhere on the face
of this earth
it is glorious morning.

Cecil Rajendra, *taken from Song of the unsung [1]*.

The experience of change permeates our personal lives, and those of people in all parts of the world. Change can be welcome, it can be part of our natural development, it can also be painful, unwelcome, unexpected and difficult to accept. Exploration of a concept, such as change, in all its diversity, can help children make the connections between their own experience and those happening in the wider world. This theme offers the opportunity to look at the ways in which change influences lives and the ways in which people bring about change.

In the national curriculum
There are many possibilities for developing the concept *Change* in the context of the national curriculum attainment targets and programmes of study. The focus we have chosen is largely based on personal and social education/RE; geography and English. You may choose to take another focus, for example, history. The web on page 99 illustrates some of the questions raised by the theme in this book. These are by no means exhaustive.

An important emphasis in personal and social education/RE is looking at the idea of change in our own lives, exploring how change affects other people. Suggested activities for this are offered in the first pages of this theme.

Opportunities are offered throughout *Change* for developing each of the English ATs, in particular speaking and listening, reading and writing. Children can prepare for and interview people about their own experiences of change. Creative work about futures will help them think about realistic or imaginary possibilities. Ideas are also suggested for using stories for discussing different perspectives.

In this section, we focus on geographical skills and issues such as: exploring how the landscape changes; viewpoints on issues; how an area develops as a result of human and economic activity; land use and the conflict of interest which sometimes arises over land use; the exploitation of resources; use and misuse of natural resources and environmental issues.

The approach

This section explores ways of enabling children to gain a sense of concept, through the theme 'Change'. The approach involves building up understanding from the familiar and then using this as a basis for looking at the unfamiliar.

Structuring a concept-based theme

From the familiar to the unfamiliar

This theme aims initially to help children make sense of their personal experiences. As children are able to build up a concept by making sense of their own experiences, they can transfer that understanding and ask similar questions about things outside their immediate environment. This involves reviewing previous ideas, assumptions and conclusions and questioning them in the light of new findings. This questioning is a continuing process, so that their conclusions are tested and expanded, thus developing a deeper understanding of the concept. In this way concepts can be built up.

This diagram taken from *Social studies in the primary school* † shows how one issue - how the housework is shared out in the family - can be explored and the concept of the division of labour developed.

1 Selection of issue *How is the housework shared out in the family?*

4 Gathering and evaluating evidence *Winston's mum and dad do it differently . . . so do Tabassum's . . .*

2 Considering own experiences *At home my mum does the washing up and dad does the drying.*

3 Developing a tentative hypothesis about the issue *All mums and dads share the jobs.*

7 Extending their enquiries beyond their immediate experience *In some Victorian families neither the mother nor the father did the housework — the servants did it.*

5 Using this evidence to test their hypothesis *We can't say all mums and dads, because . . . but lots of them . . .*

6 Making a tentative conclusion *In most of our families mums and dads share out the jobs, but in some families only one person does the work.*

10 Questioning the reliability of the evidence *Did we make it clear what we meant by 'housework'?*

8 Using new evidence to test their conclusion *We can't say work is shared in most families, because in other times and other countries . . .*

9 Making a new tentative conclusion *In Britain today . . . but this is not the general pattern because . . .*

images fairness division of labour choice bias co-operation interdependence change conflict similarity + difference development cause + consequence justice values and beliefs distribution of power communication

Concepts in theme work

The national curriculum draws on a wide range of concepts many of which can be explored across the curriculum. When one concept is the focus of the theme, others will be touched upon, thus helping children to make connections between ideas. Concepts form a sound basis for theme work for several reasons:

Global dimension

There are clearly connections between what is happening in different parts of the world. Concepts such as 'Change', 'justice' and 'division of labour' help us to make sense of our own lives, relating that understanding to those of others.

Building on children's experiences

All children come to school with a wealth of experience and interest. Within a class of thirty children there is likely to be a wide variety of experience to build on.

Open ended learning

If the children's experiences are to be taken seriously, then these will 'set the agenda' for what will go on in the classroom. This calls for an open ended, flexible and sensitive approach.

Less emphasis on knowledge

A concept-based approach can mean that the 'content' is the children's experience. Less emphasis is put on predetermined knowledge transmitted by the teacher, particularly in the early stages of concept development.

Cross curricular

Concept based themes give more scope for a cohesive cross-curricular approach.

What do we mean by concept development?

Robin Richardson argues that there are four stages to concept development. He describes these stages in terms of being able to use a word [which describes a concept] in different ways:

- **Recognising:** *being able to recognise a word in context as one that has been mentioned or seen before, one that has been talked about;*
- **Explaining:** *being able to give an explanation of that word and examples of the way it was used;*
- **Using:** *being able to use the word as part of one's own active vocabulary, whether in writing or in speech;*
- **Applying:** *being able to apply the word to one's own everyday life and situation, and to understand the implications of this for one's lifestyle.*

Selecting concepts

This list taken from *Social studies in the primary school* † suggests criteria for selecting concepts for theme work. Concepts should:

- *be relevant to the children;*
- *help to explain human behaviour and social experience;*
- *enable children to increase their understanding of their social [global/local]environment;*
- *be able to be supported by evidence and a variety of resources;*
- *have a lasting quality capable of application and re-application in a number of different subject disciplines.*

Suggestions of concepts which can successfully be used in primary themes, are made above.

Bringing out the issues

Controversy is part of everyday life; children are faced with issues inside and outside of the classroom. Learning to respond thoughtfully to issues is an important part of growing up and needs to be part of the school curriculum.

In the life of the classroom, there will be many incidental opportunities to discuss issues spontaneously as they arise. These are valuable moments to talk with children about their real concerns about the world outside the school. Teachers who are able to drop all and seize these opportunities will know the extent of children's interest in current issues, such as the chopping down of the rainforest or South Africa. This approach needs to be complemented by exploring controversial issues as part of the planned curriculum.

'Any attempt to avoid the points of controversy would lead to a curriculum which focused on the physical environment without drawing out the social, economic and political implications of the facts uncovered.' [3]

Issues in the national curriculum
It is encouraging to see the place given to issue centred work in the national curriculum. The history attainment targets for example, encourage an exploration of perspectives and bias. Particular reference to issues is made in 'Geography for ages 5-16' [4] in attainment targets 2, 3 and 4. These require children to

'explain how the landscape of the locality has been changed by human actions'; [4/4c]

'examine and give an account of an important issue that has arisen from changes or proposed changes in a tropical or subtropical locality'; [4/4d]

'compare some of the different viewpoints arising from the issue studied for 4/4d and present their own conclusions'; [4/4e].

Other geographical attainment targets also focus on issues.

Brick

...YOU KNOW IT MAKES SENSE.

Planning for an issue centred curriculum
Most themes can be planned so that issues are addressed. Within themes such as *Clothes, Ourselves* and *Change* there are potentially many controversial issues to draw out. Take, for example, a theme on transport. Instead of only looking at transport through history, look at local transport issues of the day. What do local people feel about the bus service? Do exhaust fumes affect the environment? Is the city designed for cars or for people? Who decides on local transport developments? Do local people have a say? Is it safe to go on foot? Ideas for planning an issue centred theme around an object can be found on page 11.

Through issue centred theme work, it is important that children:

- gain some understanding that people hold different points of view and explore why this is so;
- examine conflicts of interest;
- compare the vested interests different groups have in a situation;
- build up empathy with people both in familiar and different situations;
- recognise their own attitudes and what influences them;
- understand the difference between fact and opinion;
- understand that we hold images;
- begin to ask questions such as why and how?;
- collect, interpret, evaluate, analyse and present evidence;
- listen to other ideas;
- make judgements and decisions based on these;
- become confident in their own opinion and argue ideas;
- develop skills in detecting bias and recognising stereotypes;
- explore issues and concepts, such as: rights, justice and fairness, equality, power, decision making processes, priorities, choices, interdependence, cause and consequence, and exploitation.

are there things which can never be changed?

are there changes which are outside your power?

can you find stories which explore the idea of change?

what might you do to bring about change?

where are the conflicts of interest?

are there people in the news who struggle for change?

in your own life?

in school?

in the world?

if a tourist resort develops who benefits and who loses?

can you find examples of people who have pioneered change?

what changes would you like to see take place?

what can you find out about change in another place?

why did they do it?

Change

how did they bring about change?

what have been the main changes in your life?

was there a price to pay?

what has influenced these changes?

how might they have felt about it?

what has changed about the place you live in your lifetime?

which changes are permanent and which are temporary?

in your parents' lifetime?

how might it feel if you are one of the few women doing a job which traditionally has been done by men?

in the longer term past?

how does it feel when things change?

what evidence can you find for this?

what changes about your body and what stays the same?

who might you talk to - where might you look?

how might these changes affect the people who live in your area?

99

The theme : Change

Children can build up their understanding of the concept 'change' by looking at the experiences of other people. This is a chance to explore attitudes and perceptions. It also can act as a vehicle for challenging ideas without becoming too personal. Suggestions are made for extending this understanding into new situations.

Science

Science investigations can be a useful way into exploring children's understanding of change as they allow children to observe, investigate and record concrete changes in materials. Look at how substances change when they are heated or cooled. The theme also offers a context for discussing how bodies change and for sex education.

Faces

Pictures of faces are a useful and widely available resource for drawing out children's attitudes and perceptions about other people. Make your own class collection of faces ensuring that you include images of people in different parts of the world. See page 82 for possible sources. Take a film of your class; most children respond well to using photographs of themselves in discussions. Different interpretations of a photograph by the subject and the viewer forms the basis of an interesting discussion.

Changes

Give each group a photograph of a person and ask them to talk about what kind of person they think this is. They may want to talk about personality, age, role, interests, family situation etc. When they have 'created' a person, ask them to brainstorm* a list of changes that the person might have experienced; wild ideas should be encouraged as this may stop children from forming narrow stereotypes of people. When produced, the children can underline the changes which they think could actually have happened to the person in the picture.

The next stage is to think about the order in which those changes may have taken place. Some may logically have to precede others; for instance, if one of the changes is having a first baby this will obviously have to precede that child breaking a leg in a football match. Making a timeline* of changes helps clarify this.

What do you think caused the different changes?
What are the likely long term consequences of the changes?
What do you think the person feels about those changes?
Do you think any of the changes were natural?

Stories/role play*

These are both useful techniques for identifying with other people and bringing out ideas about change. Groups could create a story around a face entitled *'The day my life changed'* and write their own group story. Try this with faces from different parts of the world, to raise discussion about perceptions.

A similar activity could be devised around a role play* interview. In pairs, one person is the interviewer and the other selects a face. The task of the interviewer is to find out about the changes that have taken place in the person's life. The person with the face has to imagine him/herself to be that person and imagine what kind of changes s/he has experienced. While s/he is getting into role, the interviewer can plan questions to ask.

Moods of faces

This activity is designed to help children reflect on other people's moods and to recognise that moods change. You may need to do some work prior to this, which expands the children's vocabulary of moods as these can often be limited to angry, sad and happy. Each pair has one face. Ask them to look at it closely and then try and answer the following questions:

*   *What do you think this person is feeling?*
*   *What has caused this feeling?*
*   *How long have they been feeling like this?*
*   *What do you think they will be feeling in an hour's time?*

Statements and pictures

Groups are given a selection of statements like the ones shown here and some pictures of faces. Their task is to match the statements with the most suitable face. This will involve the children discussing their ideas and perceptions of the people behind the faces. Pairs could form fours and explain their ideas to each other.

An important change in my life was:

*   *getting the lead part in the school play;*
*   *learning to ride a BMX;*
*   *having a new baby brother;*
*   *getting a job;*
*   *learning to drive;*
*   *having my hair dyed pink;*
*   *having a letter printed in the newspaper;*
*   *getting married;*
*   *making a new friend;*
*   *moving house;*
*   *getting 10 out of 10 for maths.*

Exploring personal change

The activities designed to be used with faces can introduce children to some of the changes which people often experience. This can help to create an atmosphere in which children feel secure about exploring the changes that are happening to them.

All children will have experiences of change, it is important that we are sensitive to the fact that some children may not want to bring their home experiences into the classroom.

What changes about you?
Some things about us are constant, others change. Each child could fill in a chart like this in order to think about those things that do or do not change. The class may have common answers for some questions and different ones for others depending on their experience.

These things Change :	always	some-times	never
height		✓	
friends			✓
beliefs			
gender			
clothes			
school			
eye colour			
hair colour			
moods			
family			
personality			

Changing moods
This activity could build on the 'moods of faces' activity by helping children to explore their own moods and how those change. Ask everyone to turn to their neighbour and complete a sentence like these: 'In the last week I felt excited when.......' or 'In the dark I feel.....'.

Pairs could then discuss what they did on different days of the last week and then each write a sentence in the appropriate balloon of their own sheet. If it is too difficult to recall last week, they could fill it in at the end of each day. When completed, small groups could discuss the finished sheets and see if there are any similar experiences. Do you think certain things make us change moods? If so, what are they?

Baby photos
Many children will have photos of themselves as a baby or at a younger age. Run a quiz in which they have to try and guess who is who. How do they recognise their friends as babies? Are there features which have not changed? Children could either make a list of the changes in their own lives since the photograph was taken, or they could do it for a friend.

Influential changes
This activity is designed to help identify the changes that influence our lives. Ask the children to select five of the most important changes on their list, to write each on a slip of paper, then order them from most to least influential. Pairs or small groups could compare their findings. By the nature of this task, children may reveal personal information, which will need to be dealt with sensitively. It is also appropriate for children to retain their privacy and personal space by either opting out of the activity or selecting only those events which they are prepared to discuss.

Children could draw a timeline* of changes that have taken place in their lives. A timeline projected into the future could help them think about what kinds of changes they would like to see happening to them or, being more realistic, the changes that are likely to happen.

Change often occurs as a result of an event. Discuss what would happen if:

*   *your gran came to live with you, or*
*   *you move from the country to the city, or*
*   *a new shopping centre is built near your home, or*
*   *one of your parents loses their job.*

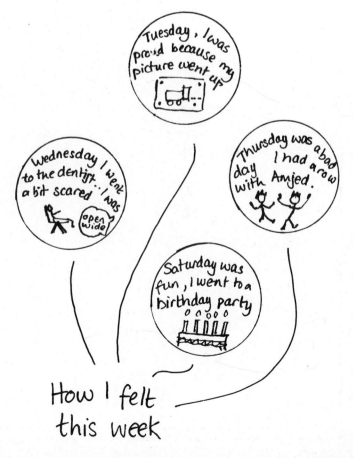

From the past

Children's understanding can be built on by looking at the changes that take place over a period of time.

Before and after

'Before and after' photographs are a useful stimulus for looking at change. Areas to focus on might be:

- *the time lapse between photographs;*
- *the cause of the change;*
- *the likely consequence of the change;*
- *different types of change such as temporary/permanent; natural/unnatural; intentional/unintentional; etc.*

Children could take their own 'before and after' photographs in the same spot with different time lapses. You may have photographs of a garden or park in different seasons or you may want to take a modern photograph to complement a scene taken several years ago. Old postcards, available from public libraries are an ideal resource for this.

Work patterns

As part of this exploration of change, the children could look at changes in work patterns using photographs of people working in non traditional roles. The *Working now* [5] pack offers a good selection. Give each group of children a photograph of someone at work and ask them to make up a name for this person and describe what they are doing. One of the activities suggested in the *Working now* booklet, *'A day in the life of...'* is a useful vehicle for familiarising the children with what might be involved in a day's work.

Ask the children to think about what it was like when the people first took up the job. What sort of things might others have said to them? For example, if they were the first person of their sex in that workplace, did people comment on this? The children could draw a timeline* for their person for the duration of their working life and highlight the changes that have happened to them. The timeline could also show possible and probable futures as shown here.

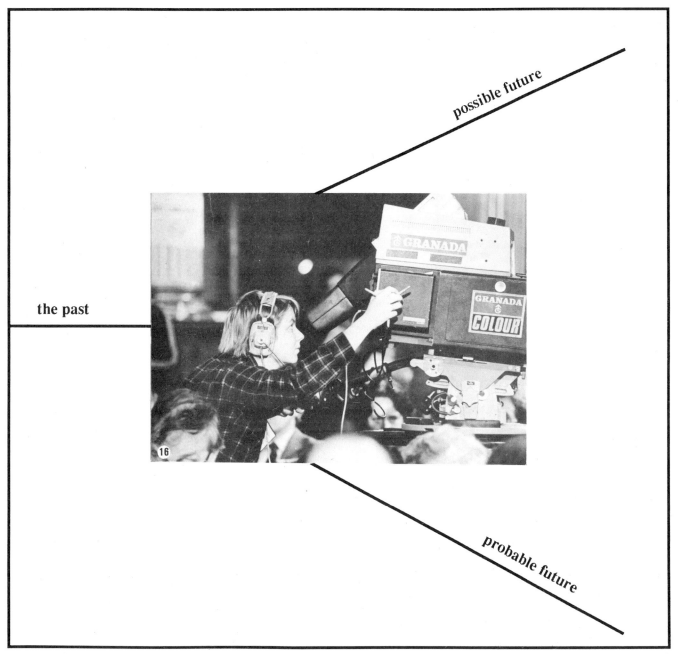

possible future

the past

probable future

Listening to visitors

Schools often invite people in to talk to the children. If organised well and the children are actively involved in the planning, this can be a valuable experience for all.

Parents and grandparents often have fascinating stories to tell which illuminate the changes that have occurred over time. This also offers a good opportunity to involve the local community in schools on the basis of their expertise, rather than as another pair of hands.

Grandparents and parents who were born and raised in another part of the world will not only be able to talk about changes over time but also over distance. They could tell you about what changes they immediately saw when they first came to this country. Can you locate where they were born on a world map? Ideas could be developed around the 'Roots and journeys' theme.

Planning a visit
First the children need to decide who they are going to invite into schools and why. This active involvement should get them excited about who is coming! Prior to the visit, they need to decide how the visitor is to be welcomed. This is a useful exercise in thinking abut how to welcome people and make them feel at ease. Role play* it, if this helps.

The children need to prepare the questions they want to ask the visitor. Groups brainstorm* a list and select which they would most like to ask and share these with others in the class, ensuring a variety of questions are ready to be asked. In doing this the children will be thinking about what they would most like to hear about. Finally, get the children to plan how the questions are going to be asked.

And afterwards....
What did the children learn? Ask them to brainstorm* what they remember from the visit, then focus on a question like 'What surprised you?' You might also want to evaluate the process of the visit. How did you think it went? How might we do it differently next time?

Interviews
Children can also conduct their own interviews. It is important they decide first what they are trying to find out about. The sheet opposite has been designed to help them do this. They will probably need supervision at first to use it. The planning process will probably influence the success of the interview. The interview needs to be flexible so it is good if children see these only as guidelines not as rigid rules to follow. Finally, they will have to decide how they are going to share their findings and what they have learnt from the process of interviewing.

A visitor
One of the teachers at the school had recently had a baby and come back to work soon afterwards. Her husband, Mr Yeomans, had given up his paid work to look after the baby. The class invited him to come into school and to talk about this.

Before the visit the children worked in groups to decide which questions they were going to ask him. Finally it was organised so that each person had one question to ask. On the day of the interview, one person acted as chair, organising the order of questioning. These are some of the issues which came up:

- What is it like to have stopped working?
- What do you do when you are looking after the baby?
- Was anything wrong with the baby when he was born?
- Why did you decide to look after the baby?
- How do you change the baby's nappy when you go into town?

After everyone had asked their initial question, there was an open discussion. In some senses this raised more interesting questions than the prepared ones, probably because the situation was real and questions more naturally came to mind.

We felt that the children had been very interested to meet Mr Yeomans, but we wondered whether they would have asked the same questions of a woman.

Some hints for interviewing........

✱ What do you want to find out about? ✱✱✱

Who is the best person to talk to? _____. Contact this person and make a time and place for the interview _____.

✱ Now plan your questions

You will need about 30 slips of paper and something to write with.

- Brainstorm - as many questions as you can think of and write one on each slip of paper

Beware! don't ask questions which can be answered by 'yes' or 'no'. Begin with words such as when, why where, how, which ....

▷ Remember ✱ ✱ ✱ this is what you wanted to find out about, so take out any questions which are not to the point.

✱ Choose ten questions

You may have too many questions - check them, then together choose the ten you want to ask. Put them in order of importance.

✱ The interview:

Who is going to ask the questions? - one person? - all of you? →

decide who is going to ask which questions and in what order.

How are you going to record the answers?
   If you are going to use a tape recorder.. ask the person if they don't mind!

✱ Afterwards...

What are you going to do with the information? / write about it / tell the class ??

How did the interview go?   jot down the good points and bad points.
When you interview someone else, how will you do it differently?

Where the forest meets the sea

Stories are a very useful medium through which to raise all kinds of issues. More and more books are being published which can be used in this way throughout the primary age range. This is how you could use one story to look at the issue of change and tourism with young children.

Where the forest meets the sea† is the story of a young boy who, with his father, visits an island off the coast of Australia by boat for the day. He wanders through the rainforest and imagines what life has been like in the past. As they plan to leave at the end of the day, they imagine what the future might be and conjure up the image of a tourist town. The book is beautifully illustrated. It offers lots of opportunities for work on the past, present and future.

Having read the story, an initial activity could involve brainstorming* the changes that might have taken place in the rainforest since prehistoric times. How much has it changed? What has caused those changes? Will other situations have changed more over that period of time?

'But will the forest still be there when we come back?'
The final page leaves us with this poignant question. The image of tourism is superimposed on that of the quiet island. This gives scope for discussing whether this offers a good future or not.

Introduce the discussion by a 'What do you know - what do you want to know?'* activity about tourism. Build on this using the statements on the opposite page which show how people who may be involved in tourism might see the situation. Children could work in groups, first sorting* the cards into two piles, those who think tourism is a good idea and those who don't. Can they sort again using different criteria? Then they each take a different role card and role play* a discussion giving the viewpoint of the person on the card. Alternatively, they could try and draw out of the statements both advantages and disadvantages of tourism.

- *Are these changes for the better?*
- *Why have they taken place?*
- *Who do they benefit?*

The children could then think about what other futures they would hope for, for the island. They could draw a timeline* from prehistoric times to the present day and into the future, or draw their mental map* of the future. For other material about tourism, see the resources section. Tourism Concern [see address on page 111] supply a useful newsletter.

Changing stories/Making stories†
If you want to look more generally at how stories themselves change over a period of time and space, these two resources from the ILEA English Centre offer practical ideas.

from Where the forest meets the sea.

Hotel owner

This island has been a great discovery, a real paradise island. We've now built 4 hotels and more and more people are coming each year. Business is booming; we're planning to build a disco and roller skating park soon. Some people have criticised us for coming to this spot, but I think beautiful places should be for everyone, not just the locals. We have created work for the island people in the hotels and they are grateful to us. Civilisation has come here at last.

The conservationist

My job is to make sure that the environment on the island is not destroyed by tourism. In other places where hotels have been built the wildlife has been destroyed, the sea has become polluted and the breeding places for animals disturbed. I am concerned that the same will happen here unless we are very careful.

Old islander

This is our island; my people have lived here for generations, hunting, fishing, farming. We have always lived in peace with the land and animals. We wake with the sun and sleep when it goes down. The stories and traditions of our ancestors are passed from parents to children. We have lived simply until the bulldozers and cement mixers came, the noisy workers and half-naked holiday makers. What kind of future is this for my grandchildren?

The boy

I remember visiting the island as a boy with my father. I wandered through the forest, listening to the birds and animals and insects. It seemed like I had walked back in time and that I could imagine the dinosaurs and other prehistoric animals. Now the island has changed; the holiday makers have no respect for the forest. They sit on the beach or take pleasure cruises around the bay. Each day a Land Rover will take a group of them into the forest, but they take the same route and the Land Rover tracks are wearing away the soil.

The waiter

I was born on the island but went away when I was 7 to the mainland to boarding school. I came back for holidays but found the island too quiet. I missed television and the things of the city. Now I work here, in a hotel serving food and drinks. I don't like wearing the silly uniform but the job brings in good money. I'm saving up for a car.

Holiday maker

This is a good place for a holiday - to really get away from it all. The kids love it. You can do anything you want - eating, drinking, lying by the pool, taking a safari into the jungle. We enjoy getting out of the city to different resorts. There's plenty for the children to do with the funfair, the swimming pool and the organised games. I'm going to tell my friends to come here.

The musician

I learnt to play my instrument as a small child, my family taught me the traditional songs and rhythms. My talent is respected by my people. When the hotels were built, the owners advertised for a local musician to entertain at night. I thought that the tourists would like my music so I took the job. But my music isn't like their's. I have to change my tunes. I play what they want to hear, they think it's traditional island music, but I know it isn't.

Chico Mendes

Chico Mendes was born in 1944 on a rubber estate in north west Brazil. He became the leader of the rubber tappers in their fight to stop the Amazon rainforest from being destroyed.

As a child, he learnt how to 'tap' latex [liquid rubber] from rubber trees. The day began at dawn when the rubber tappers made a cut in each tree in their patch and left a cup to catch the latex. Later in the day they collected the latex and prepared it for sale.

Chico didn't learn to read and write as a child. He got the chance to learn when he was 18. Every Saturday afternoon, Chico would walk for three hours through the forest to a hut, and there he learnt to read using old newspapers. For the first time, he found out what was happening in his country and in the outside world.

Being able to read and write made a huge difference. He learnt that the rainforest was being destroyed by rich landowners to make money and that this affected the people who lived and worked in the forest and also the climate of the world.

The landowners would clear the forest so they could graze cattle later to be killed for tinned beef. They would sell the wood from the trees to America or Europe for hardwood furniture.

The climate in the rainforest is hot and moist. The forest is rich in plant and animal life but if this is disturbed most species are unable to live outside it. Once the rainforest is uprooted, plants and animals die and the soil is of little use for grazing.

Chico Mendes decided that something had to be done to change the situation. He formed a local trade union. This organised *empates*, or 'stand ins'. When they heard that a patch of forest was to be cleared, men, women and children would gather together on the site and persuade the hired workers, paid by the landowners, who were cutting down the trees to leave. The local people were sometimes shot at or threatened with violence, but they tried to resist without fighting back.

Chico knew that education had been very important for him, so he worked with others to set up schools for children and adults to learn to read and write. Organisations like Oxfam and Christian Aid helped fund these schools. The Brazilian government only gave a little money; they feared that education would make people dissatisfied.

In 1985 Chico was at the National Rubber Tappers Congress which urged the government to look at
- the needs and rights of the peoples living in the rainforest;
- the future of the rainforest itself.

They wanted the government to see the rainforest as an immense natural resource. They suggested that 'extractive reserves' should be set up, where rubber tappers could live and work. They wanted a better price for their rubber. As people in different parts of the world heard about Chico and the rubber tappers, they lobbied for change.

Chico and the rubber tappers met with the Indians living in the forest. For years these two groups had fought each other but now they realised that they needed to work together to bring about the change they both wanted.

All the time, Chico found there was a threat from the landowners. Often the government and the police were on their side. They had money and power; but the peoples of the forest struggled on to defend the rainforest.

On 22nd December 1988 Chico Mendes was shot dead, by men hired by the landowners.

Brazil and the world was shocked by this news. Chico had spent his life getting his people to agree on the need for change and to work together for that change. He said "the struggle teaches us many things, everyday we learn something new. Our roots are too deep for us to think of giving up the struggle".

Based on the account in *Fight for the forest*†.

Action for change

Change comes about in all kinds of ways. Sometimes it is an organic process, at other times it comes after years of struggle to fulfil a vision or dream. This page looks at action for change which the children can take and examples of action that have been taken.

One of the most striking things about many of the development projects in countries of the South is that people are pulling together to define what changes they want to see taking place and then working to put them into effect. The images regularly held in this country of passive receivers of aid need to be challenged.

Introduce the idea that people work for change by looking at examples of campaigns or struggles. Assemblies are often a useful forum for looking at the lives of famous people who have fought for changes. Give modern examples; black people as well as white and women as well as men.

Chico Mendes
The story of Chico Mendes and the fight of the rubbers tappers to save the Amazon rainforest is a moving story. Photocopy the account opposite to use with children. Before they start, the children could do a 'What do we know, what do we want to know?'* activity. Then ask groups to list the ways Chico Mendes used to bring about change. Which do they think are the most important? Role play* the rubber tappers meeting the landowners.

A rainforest child† and *Science for survival* [6] will support a further exploration of the issue of the destruction of the rainforests. Children can investigate the importance of soil and the danger of soil erosion, through scientific experiments.

Zeynep - that really happened to me†
This book tells the story of how an infants school in Hackney fought a campaign to stop the deportation of the family of two of its children, Zeynep and Fatih Hasbudak. Because the parents were born outside Britain, the Home Office ordered that they leave the country; Zeynep and her brother could stay because they were born in Britain, however this would mean splitting the family. The story told in drawings, photographs and words reveals how the campaign unfolded.

Read the children the book. You may want to do some activities familiarising children with the story, e.g sequencing key events, drawing timelines*, photograph activities*, etc. When the children are clear about what happened, ask them in groups to discuss why the campaign was launched and to list all the people involved. The class can brainstorm* what strategies were used during this campaign [writing letters, making banners, getting publicity, demonstrating, raising money, collecting signatures, holding meetings, supporting the family etc.]. They could then add any other campaigning strategies they know of. The process of studying *Zeynep* is likely to raise issues about rights of residency in Britain, racism and the right to campaign.

In the end the campaign failed and Zeynep returned to Turkey with her family. Some teachers have expressed concern about

this and have suggested that this is a reason for not using this book. Real life stories do not always have happy endings, but the story goes on. One way of coping with the disappointment is to look into the future drawing a timeline* from the end of the book for the next ten years projecting what might happen. A further discussion of how you might use *Zeynep* can be found in *Do it justice!*†

Action
You might find that the children want to take some action for change themselves, this may be on an issues close to their experiences, such as bullying in the playground, or it may arise out of concern for something in another part of the world. Set up an activity which involves brainstorming* the changes the children would like to see take place. If groups do this, they could then categorize these changes into:

> *those they can do something about*
> *those they can't do anything about.*

A useful discussion might evolve around what they think they cannot change, why that is and whether there is anyone who could make those changes. Are certain changes easier to make if there is a group of you involved?

Taking the first list, ask the children to pick out two and talk about how they would go about effecting change. If some of these relate to the classroom or school, have a go at implementing those that are practical. The whole process of deciding to take action and following it through is a valuable one for children. It will help them understand about the time involved in collective decision making processes, the difficulties in agreeing and the final feelings of achievement or disappointment.

Zeynep - that really happened to me.

Resources: Change

The rainforest child, an active learning pack for 8-13 year olds, Greenlight Publications,1989.
A cross curricular pack which looks at issues of development in tropical rainforest. The materials are designed to be used with the national curriculum, in particular science, technology, maths and English.

Changing stories, ILEA English Centre, 1984.
Bias in fairy tales is an interesting theme to follow with children. This teacher's handbook contains ideas and photocopiable pages to use with children to get discussion going about how fairytales teach us about stereotyped roles.

Conflict, change and our future, a teaching pack for the middle years, F. Nicholas,1983, available from EARO, The Resources and Technology Centre, Back Hill, Ely, Cambs.
This pack focuses on the themes of conflict and change and explores ways in which children can explore conflicts within their own experience and in the wider world. It looks at change and the future: what kinds of changes do children hope for? The pack contains teaching activities as well as stimulus sheets for children.

Do it justice! resources and activities for introducing education in human rights, DEC, 1988.
A handbook containing resources and strategies for teaching for human rights. Reference is made to over 100 titles - children's stories, novels, handbooks and packs with ideas for exploring issues of rights. Many teachers find human rights education a useful angle from which to approach issues of race, gender, disability etc.

Fight for the forest, Chico Mendes in his own words, Latin America Bureau, 1989.
A powerful testament to the life of Chico Mendes, revealing how local forest peoples are leading the worldwide fight to save Amazonia.

Hidden messages? activities for exploring bias, DEC, 1986.
Books which children read contain hidden messages, through words, visuals and information which is included or omitted. These biases can influence children's attitudes and perceptions. This book suggests how you can raise primary children's awareness about different types of bias e.g. by looking at stereotypes, language, fairy tales etc.

Making stories, ILEA English Centre, 1984.
Ideas for discussing the construction of folk tales with children are contained in this teachers' handbook. One example looks at stories which appear in a slightly altered form in different places. What causes a story to change over time and space?

Science for survival - plants and rainforests in the classroom, Adam Cade, WWF, 1988.
Taking the Malaysian rainforest as the main focus, this handbook looks at the science of plants and their links with people in their natural environments. Designed for secondary teachers; some of the investigations about the importance of roots are easily adaptable for the primary classroom.

Stories in the multilingual classroom, ILEA Learning Resources, 1983.
This book explores the special role of stories in the multilingual classroom. It focuses on the ways in which they can be used to support children's learning of English as a second language and how this can be done as part of everyday work, with a value for all children.

Nobody's family is going to change, Louise Fitzhugh, MacMillan, 1978.
Set in a Black American family, Emma wants to become a lawyer like her father; her brother Willie wants to be a dancer. Both meet resistance from their parents and air their frustrations that nothing looks as if its going to change. In the end, Emma works out her own response to this. A useful story for looking at how you can bring about change and the frustrations involved in waiting.

Social studies in the primary school, ILEA Curriculum Guidelines, 1980.
Ideas for developing social studies around concepts and enquiry based learning are addressed alongside strategies for planning at school and classroom level.

Where the forest meets the sea, Jeannie Baker, Walker Books/Julia MacRae, 1987.
A boy and his father take a boat to a remote island off the coast of Queensland in Australia. The reflections of the boy on the past and on possible futures are illustrated in relief collage and photographs.

Zeynep - that really happened to me, Zeynep Hasbudak and Brian Simons, ALTARF, 1986.
The true story of how an infants school in London fought a campaign to stop the deportation of the family of two of its children. The story told in photographs, words and drawings, addresses issues of racism and rights in a way that is accessible to young children.

Journals

These are some useful magazines and journals which contain articles and resources to support theme work.

Dragon's Teeth
A journal which examines racism and children's books, in education and in the media. It contains useful news and reviews. Available from, NCRCB, 5 Cornwall Crescent, The Basement Office, London W11 1PH.

Issues in race and education
As its title suggests, this magazine looks at some of the questions raised concerning racism in schools. Available from: 'Issues' 75 Alkham Road, London N16 6XE

Junior education/Child education
Aimed at junior and infant teachers respectively, these magazines are a useful update on curriculum debates, project work and book reviews. Available from: Scholastic Publications Ltd., 9 Parade, Leamington Spa, Warwickshire CV32 4DG.

Multicultural teaching
A regular journal containing issues and debates about multi-cultural/anti-racist education. Available from: Trentham Books, Unit 13/14, Trent Trading Park, Botteslow St., Stoke on Trent,ST1 3LY.

Questions, exploring science and technology 3-13
A practical monthly magazine for primary teachers offering suggestions for investigations in the classroom. Available from: 6/7 Hockley Hill, Hockley, Birmingham B18 5AA.

The New Internationalist
A monthly magazine which explores development issues. It is invaluable background reading for teachers. Many of the charts, statistics and case studies can be adapted for use in the classroom. Available from: 120-126 Lavender Avenue, Mitcham, Surrey CR4 3HP.

Useful addresses

Afro Caribbean Education Resources Project [ACER]
Wyvil School
Wyvil Road
London
SW8 2TJ

CAFOD
2 Romero Close
Stockwell Road
London
SW9 9TY

Christian Aid
PO Box 100
London
SE1 7RT

Development Education Centre [Birmingham]
Selly Oak Colleges
Bristol Road
Birmingham
B29 6LE

Earth education - U.K.
Co-ordinator: Ian Duckworth
Ufton Court Centre
Green Lane
Nervet
Berks
RG7 4HD

Equal Opportunities Commission
Overseas House
Quay Street
Manchester
M3 3HN

Harcourt, Brace, Jovanovitch
[new distributers for many of the ILEA materials]
Foots Cray High Street
Sidcup
Kent
DA14 5HP

Letterbox Library
8 Bradbury Street
London
N16 8JN

National Association. of Development Education Centres [NADEC]
6 Endsleigh Street
London
WC1X ODX
Please ask for the address of your local DEC.

National Writing Project and the National Oracy Project
Newcombe House
45 Notting Hill Gate
London W11 3JB

Oxfam Education Department
274 Banbury Road
Oxford
OX2 7DZ

Save the Children Fund
Mary Datchelor House
17 Grove Lane
Camberwell
London
SE5 8RD

Trocaire
169 Booterstown Avenue,
Blackrock
Co. Dublin
Ireland

Tourism Concern
c/o 8 St Mary's Terrace
Ryton
Tyne and Wear
NE40 3Al

UNICEF
55 Lincoln's Inn Fields
London
WC2A 3NB

Worldwide Fund for Nature
Panda House
Weyside Park
Godalming
Surrey GU7 1XR

References

Introduction
1. Ange Grunsell, North London Oxfam primary education unit.
2. Children and race ten years on, D. Milner, Ward Lock Educational, 1983.
3. Task group on assessment and testing: a report, DES and Welsh Office, 1987.
4. From policy to practice, DES, 1989.
5. Criteria for Assessment in Teacher Education.
6. The Earl of Arran Government spokesperson in the Lords on Clause 1 of the Education Reform Bill, Hansard 21 June 1988.
7. Based on questions from: Curriculum in action - practical classroom evaluation, P234, The Open University, 1982.
8. Behind the scenes, photographs and inservice activities for exploring the hidden curriculum, DEC, 1988.
9. A chapter entitled 'A whole school approach', A. Grunsell and C. Ross in 'Making global connections, World Studies 8-13', M. Steiner and D. Hicks, Oliver and Boyd, 1989.

Children working together
1. Co-operative group work, J. Sprackling, Manchester City Council Education Department.
2. National Oracy Project reports, see address list on page 111.
3. World Studies 8-13, a teachers' handbook, S. Fisher and D. Hicks, page 15, Oliver and Boyd, 1985.
4. A sense of school - an active learning approach to inservice, DEC, 1986.
5. Behind the scenes, photographs and inservice activities for exploring the hidden curriculum, DEC, 1988.
6. Learning to teach through discussion, J. Rudduck, Centre for Applied Research in Education, 1979.
7. 8.11 in the non statutory guidance for English, Key stage 1.
8. Get the picture! developing visual literacy in the infant classroom, M. Davies, DEC 1989.
9. What is a family? photographs and activities, DEC 1990.
10. Doing things in and about the home, Maidenhead Teacher's Centre, Trentham books, 1983/7.
11. Doorways, IYSH, Ikon Productions, 1987.
12. Working now, photographs and activities for exploring gender roles in the primary classroom, DEC, 1989.

What is a country
1. Dove on fire, poems on peace, justice and ecology, Cecil Rajendra, World Council of Churches, 1987.
2. The Interim report - Geography Working Group, 3.18 DES and the Welsh Office, 1989.
3. The changing world in the primary school, B. Clark, CWDE, 1979.
4. Censoring reality, Beverley Naidoo, ILEA Centre for Anti-racist Education, 1984.
5. Hidden messages? activities for exploring bias, DEC, 1986.
6. Criteria for the evaluation of racism in textbooks and children's literature, World Council of Churches.
7. World Studies 8-13, a teachers' handbook, S. Fisher and D. Hicks, Oliver and Boyd, 1985.

Roots and journeys
1. Dove on fire, poems on peace, justice and ecology, Cecil Rajendra, World Council of Churches, 1987.
2. Water - photographs, case studies and activities, DEC, 1990.
3. 4.21 in the Final report, National curriculum, history working group, April 1990.
4. 3.28 in the Final report, National curriculum, history working group, April 1990.

5. Science for survival - plants and rainforests in the classroom, Adam Cade, WWF, 1988.
6. Self esteem- a classroom affair, Michele and Craig Borba, Harper and Row, 1982.
7. City images - priorities for development, DEC, 1990.
8. Black makers of history series, Peckham Publishing Project, 1988.
9. World Studies 8-13, a teachers' handbook, S. Fisher and D. Hicks, Oliver and Boyd, 1985.
10. The languages book, M. Simons, ILEA English Centre, 1981.
11. Making stories, ILEA English Centre, 1984.

Images
1. Dove on fire, poems on peace, justice and ecology, Cecil Rajendra, World Council of Churches, 1987.
2. Children's images of other countries - the influence of the media, M. Storm. UNESCO research carried out by Lambert and Klineberg. Referred to in an article in The changing world in the primary school, B. Clark, CWDE, 1979.
3. Children's images of third world countries, Janet Graham and Susan Lynn, South Bank polytechnic.
4. Visualising anti-racism, an article in Issues in race and education, Spring 1985.

Change
1. Song of the unsung, poems on unpoetic issues like war, want and refugees, Cecil Rajendra, World Council of Churches, 1983.
2. Learning for change in a world society, reflections, activities and resources, R. Richardson, the World Studies Project, page 109, 1976.
3. Have you considered? an article in Issues in race and education no. 51, Summer 1987.
4. AT 4 level 4, Geography for ages 5-16 - proposals of the Secretary of State for Education and Science and the Secretary of State for Wales, DES and the Welsh Office, June 1990.
5. Working now, photographs and activities for exploring gender roles in the primary classroom, DEC, 1989.
6. Science for survival - plants and rainforests in the classroom, Adam Cade, WWF, 1988.